Do You
Honestly
Want To Grow
House Plants?

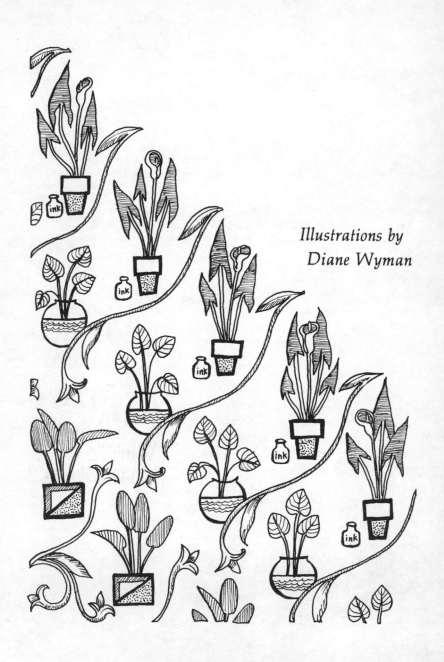

Illustrations by
Diane Wyman

Do You Honestly Want To Grow House Plants?

Brian Murphy
"the plant doctor"

Dent Canada

Copyright © 1976

by J. M. DENT & SONS (CANADA) LIMITED

ISBN   0-460-91094-9

Printed in Canada

Canadian Cataloguing in Publication Data

```
Murphy, Brian.
  Do you honestly want to grow house plants?

Bibliography: p.
Includes index.
ISBN 0-460-91094-9 pa.


1. House plants.  I. Title.

SB419.M87       635.9'65       C76-017104-1
```

Contents

Coffee

Maranta
(prayer plant)

Introduction

A friend came to visit me from England a few years ago, and while she and her husband were here we would have breakfast together each morning. My friend is one of those renowned poor wakers. Every day, at breakfast, this normally very beautiful and cheerful person would sit glowering in her chair with half-closed eyes and hunched shoulders, making grumbling noises until she had had at least three cups of the blackest coffee — a real case of Dr Jekyll and Mr Hyde!

In the centre of my dining-room table stood a fluffy little Maranta, its leaves sticking out in all directions, proudly brandishing their colourful markings. To my friend, 'plants' meant only those sick-looking Sansevierias and rubber trees in dentists' waiting rooms; she didn't like plants, and I'm sure she secretly thought I was nuts. Anyhow, for whatever reason (I'm sure a psychiatrist would know — maybe something to do with her Grade 4 teacher), she would release all her early morning fire on my poor, defenceless, lovable little Maranta. She would say, 'What the #%Z*&! are you so cheery about this morning, you stupid plant?' Sometimes she would threaten it with physical violence, by suggesting she water it with boiling coffee; she would 'accidentally' drop plates nearby, or hide her ashtray under a large leaf. As this daily ritual continued, my Maranta never did complain: instead, it flowered.

And the reason for this little story? In the end, by its persistently cheerful and lively greenness, my Maranta single-handedly won my friend's heart; so much so that her small London apartment is now full to the brim with plants. The fact is, everyone likes the look and feel and smell of living, growing plants. For no matter who you are, once you have been subjected to indoor plants, it's only a matter of time before you end up with lots of them in your home.

1

Home Away from Home

It rained so much yesterday—sheets of water smashed down onto the vegetation of the jungle, soaking everything. The fat raindrops exploded as they hit the branches of the highest trees, their offspring bursting out in all directions, continuing the path downwards. So much water fell just in a minute that all the plant life, down to the smallest creeper on the jungle floor, was bathed in water—water running in all directions, pouring over the deep layers of decaying leaves, filling every hollow and crevice to overflowing; and then, as quickly as it had started, the rain stopped.

The ever-present heat began to evaporate the water into steam. Droplets of water on the leaves just disappeared before our very eyes and the air felt wringing wet with moisture. The clouds then moved slowly away, allowing the searing noonday sun to raise the temperature even more. The sun was brilliant, as always; its radiance was unbelievable. Sunlight poured down through the topmost layer of vegetation as if it didn't exist, then through the second and the third all the way down to the soil itself. Though in some places at ground level the vegetation is so thick that the world seems very dark, even here mosses and creeping plants cover every square inch of ground.

By evening, all trace of the rain had vanished. As dusk turned to night the air cooled; and now, in the early hours of morning just before sunrise, everything is covered in a thick layer of shimmering dewdrops. In an hour or so the old familiar sun will be out again, lighting, heating, and drying everything—except the air.

Are you wondering what that story of a day in the jungle has to do with you? It's to help you to understand the kind of conditions our friend the house plant enjoyed in his ancestral home—the tropical rain forest.

Most house plants are tropical, and most of them grow on the forest floor. They sit under tall trees, which are matted together with vine-twisted branches. (We've all seen or heard about Tarzan movies, in which the muscular and fearless hero swings from tree to tree.) In the crooks of these trees plants live, growing on the decayed leaves that have collected there. If you stood on the jungle floor and looked up, all you would see is *green*: hardly any sky, just leaves, branches, and more leaves. Plants on the jungle floor may go through life without ever feeling the full strength of the sun—but don't misunderstand: indirect tropical sunlight is still very bright.

If you could reproduce all the conditions I mentioned in my little 'travelogue', your tropical plant would do wonderfully. It seems you have three choices: one, pack up all your furniture and belongings and move to the Amazon River Basin; two, sell your house, buy a greenhouse, and move in; three (always keeping in mind what a plant prefers), reproduce the correct conditions as best you can in your home, where you alone are Mother Nature.

Now let's concern ourselves with what we should do to help plants flourish in our homes. Four main conditions are necessary to a plant's basic happiness; in order of importance they are light, water, humidity, and warmth. If we were nasty scientific sorts, we could take four identical very healthy plants and run a controlled experiment.

Plant 1 would be watered exactly as its species requires; we would give it the correct humidity and temperature but place it in a totally dark room.

Plant 2 would be given the correct light, humidity, and temperature, but no water.

For Plants 3 and 4 we would also provide three out of the four correct conditions—but Plant 3 would receive no warmth, Plant 4 no humidity.

A fun experiment—and I'm sure it wouldn't take a Ph.D. in Horticulture to predict that all four plants would do poorly, if they didn't die outright. But our scientific experiment would tell us four things about our plants:

Plant 1, without sufficient light, would have lost all its lower leaves. All its new growth would be on long, weak stems, and its new leaves would be a pallid green colour, their sizes much smaller than the earlier healthy ones.

Plant 2, without water, would of course be all dried up, brown and withered.

Plant 3, without warmth, would still be green in colour but in a condition of total collapse—limp and wilted.

Our last friend (Plant 4), without any humidity, would still be growing, but though it would probably still have all its leaves, their edges would be brown and crisp like potato chips.

Scientists we are not. All we want to do is grow healthy green plants. At present I am sticking to the barest necessities; later on in this book I intend to deal with all the fascinating details also needed for proper plant care.

Common sense, coupled with a bit of Sherlock Holmes, is what is *really* going to make it possible for you to be a fully bona fide Grade A Green Thumb. What I would like you to do with all your plants is to try to imagine what they would experience if they were living in their natural surroundings, as well as to investigate any disaster with the care and thoroughness of a great detective. Let's say you are tenderly watering your plants and you see that one of them has a few yellow or brown leaves. Chewing your fingernails and crying is not what you should do. If you think that I, as a Plant Doctor, never have a plant suffering from brown leaves, or, for that matter, that I never lose a plant altogether, you're quite wrong! But, when my plant does get a yellow leaf, I don't just cross my fingers and hope it doesn't happen again. Instead, I investigate. That is exactly what *you* are to do. When one of your plants looks feeble, ask yourself whether you've been doing anything different to it or with it, lately. Inspect the ill-fated leaf. Check for bugs. Look to see where the leaf came from—was it a new one or an old one? Look around. How's the light? Is the room too hot or too cold? Have you been watering too much or too little? Think. When a plant begins to die, it is not because the Great Plant Demon has visited your home, it's because something is wrong. Don't despair—accept the yellow leaf as a challenge.

People who visit my home are always surprised. They expect to see a magnificent array of beautiful plants; instead, they find a motley collection of sickly greenery, struggling to survive. My home is filled with over-watered, bug-infested, undernourished specimens that I am striving to 'make good' again. To me, the repair of a sick plant is more exciting than the mere maintenance of a perfect one. To get a half-dead plant to regrow and maybe even to flower is the ultimate in satisfaction. So please, if your Croton drops half its leaves, don't unceremoniously dump it in the garbage—how about trying to do something really effective and making it grow entirely under your baton? And after a line of propaganda like that your heart must be crying out for all those poor drooping objects you gave up on in the past. If I have stirred you to really want to care for your plants, then I am happy.

Let's imagine you know absolutely nothing about plants. You are now standing in the kitchen, and on the kitchen table is the first green guy you fell in love with at the supermarket. What do we do now? First you must find a spot for

... my surprising home

him to sit—somewhere he will look nice and get enough light, for light helps plants make food: without light, no food. A safe spot as far as light is concerned is usually a windowsill, though not one that is an arm's length from your neighbour's wall, of course. The next thing we have to do is water the little brute to keep him crisp and perky. Though later on I will try to totally confuse you as to just what is the correct amount of water to give a plant, right now I am keeping it simple. The one thing you must know about watering is that you should NEVER water any plant while the soil is still wet or moist. At least wait until the surface is dry before rewatering.

Now we have started off on the right foot: our little 59¢ friend is in sufficient light, and not wilting. What now? The next job is to mist the little devil, for as we know from our day in the jungle, his ancestors thrived on the dew and moisture that prevailed there. Canada is a cold country. Cold air is a drying agent: the colder the air, the less humid it becomes. But our plants can't win, for when we turn up the furnace to combat the cold, the heat, too, dries out the air. Very hard on the plants! To prevent those brown, crisp leaf edges, we must (a) moisturize the air as best we can with a humidifier, vaporizer, pans of water sitting on radiators, or any other method we can think of; (b) mist our plants at least once a day during the winter with an atomizer —that's a grand word for 'sprayer', and you can buy one in most florists or department stores. Misting also provides an imitation rain, which helps to wash dust off the leaves; it keeps the lower stems supple, making it easier for new growing points to form.

The final comfort we must provide for your new star boarder is also the easiest—warmth. In keeping ourselves comfortable, we are also providing a livable temperature for most house plants. You have to watch out for the heating outlets themselves, though. To stand a plant on a radiator is pure folly: if you can't put your hand on one, would you expect your plant to like his feet there? He should be at least three feet away from any source of heat.

That wasn't difficult, was it? Just those few simple facts and we're off to a winning start. Though we may run into a few bumps on an otherwise smooth path, let's get on with the show.

2

$39.98 and All the Red Spiders You Can Carry

The first step to successful indoor gardening begins with the purchase of a healthy house plant. If the plant you are buying is harbouring bugs, has root rot or any other serious malady, your chances of success are limited indeed. You should always ascertain the condition of the plant you wish to buy *before* you buy it.

The owner of a plant store is obviously going to take every step to try and make his plants look so beautiful that they are sure to sell. It's common practice to spray a plant with a commercial product so that the leaves will shine, to pull off any imperfect or dead leaves, and to decorate the pot or plant with bows or coloured foil before it meets the public. A shiny young Schefflera with a pink bow and red or silver foil around its pot may look the picture of health, but lurking under the bow may be an army of incredibly hungry red spiders intent on world domination. It is your job, when purchasing a plant, to be cold and heartless. Never give in to the appeal of the bright and shiny plant until you have given it a complete physical examination.

When you are confronted by a plant that you definitely want, try to keep calm. I know what it's like when you have been looking for a particular plant for a long time. The urge to swipe your find off the table and run to the cashier is very, very hard to suppress, but to give in to it may be a fatal mistake, both for the plant you are buying and for those that you already own.

First comes leaf inspection. Ignore the shiny top; instead, turn the leaf over and look underneath, for it is the underside of the leaf that really tells you what condition the plant is in. It should have no marks or deposits of grainy materials, or bits of fluff, or bumps, or anything unusual at all, on it. The only acceptable spots that may be found on the undersides of leaves are those left by a pesticide, which is sprayed up underneath the plant to prevent red spider attacks, leaving spots of residue when it dries. If the plant you are inspecting has pesticide on it, score one point towards buying it!

After you have looked under the plant's leaves and are satisfied that they are bug free, you should then become brutal and flick some of the leaves with your finger: tap the leaf sharply from a distance of about an inch. A healthy plant will ignore this assault; however, if the leaf falls off with little resistance and no apparent 'bleeding' of sap, something is probably wrong. Perhaps it has been sprayed with a pesticide that didn't suit it, hasn't been acclimatized properly, or has root trouble. Whatever the reason, you can be sure it's not a good sign.

Now that the leaves have had their going over, it's time to check the basic structure—the branches and stems. Whatever shade of green they are, the stems, branches, or trunk of the plant should not be host to any unusual-looking splotches of brown or black. There should be no white or brown dots or lumps clinging to the stems, hiding in the angle where the leaf joins the stem, or showing at the end of the stem. In other words, the stems should look nice and clean.

Check the soil and pot next. See if the roots are showing on the surface or through the hole in the bottom. If the roots

are exposed, check to see that they are firm and crisp, not soggy, or dried out and brittle.

Lastly, check the price tag! There is a vast variety of places to buy plants, from elegantly mirrored and tastefully designed plant parlours to the corner food store or supermarket where the plants nestle between the oranges and the onions. Most of these places buy their stock from the local greenhouses or plant warehouses. Many a corner food store is carrying exactly the same size and species of plant as is the plant parlour, for both make their purchases from the same supplier. The only difference between the two is the price. If you are satisfied with the condition of a plant, you should buy it regardless of where it is for sale. Sometimes good bargains can be found at the supermarket. Though you can often benefit from the lower prices at the supermarket, the plant parlour will usually stand behind its product for a period of time—if you have unwittingly chosen a poor plant, you can return it within a reasonable length of time.

Some people who sell plants know a great deal about the plants they are selling; others, unfortunately, don't know the first thing about them, which I suppose doesn't matter if they are selling healthy plants. They sometimes label plants incorrectly and, by mistake, give wrong advice. I couldn't begin to count the number of times I have heard impossible advice given to a customer, so if advice is given to you and your new plant is labelled, fine—but don't take the verbal name or advice as law; consult your books and figure out for yourself your new plant's name and how you should look after it. It is imperative that you know the correct name and how to care for each and every one of your plants. Every plant has its own personal set of growing conditions that must be met if it is to thrive. Without knowing these, your job as a successful indoor gardener will be much more difficult.

There are a number of books that are great for identification purposes. Many of them have excellent colour photographs, and give the names of the plants as well as basic descriptions of the growing conditions they prefer. If you don't own one of these books, your local library does. In the Bibliography (page 121) I have listed some of the ones I like best, and have indicated which are perhaps the most straightforward and the simplest to use. But don't forget that newer, equally helpful, books do become available from time to time, so continue to keep your eye on your local bookstore and library.

Now let's get back to the plant store, where you have just bought your plant. The next task is to get your treasure home. Except during warm summer months, you should always insist on some type of enclosed environment to bring your plant home in. To stress that point I'll tell you a true story. One February a client of mine was moving to new offices directly across the street. Even though it was a cold day, he thought it would not hurt his plants to bring them across without covering them up; after all, they would only be outside for a minute or two at the most. Shortly after their quick run across the street, over half the plants were dead, the other half a sickly crew indeed! So, even with your plant all wrapped up nicely, don't go wandering down the street window-shopping. Get home as quickly and warmly as possible, for the longer the plant is outside, the greater the danger of frost damage.

Now that you have your new plant home, you should do two things to ensure its safety and long life—and that of your other plants. *All* new house plants, without exception, should be acclimatized and quarantined. When you acclimatize a plant, all you are trying to do is to help it adjust to its new surroundings with as little physical shock as possible. All the plants you buy have either come directly here from the south or have spent a happy life in a greenhouse. In both the greenhouse and the tropical plant farm in the south, the conditions were that of a plant heaven, where the plants enjoyed high humidity, bright filtered light, and constant warm temperatures. The differences between these conditions and those in your home are quite dramatic, and certain plants may succumb almost immediately if they are not acclimatized correctly. Place your new house plant in a spot where it will receive the brightest recommended light possible—a south window for all sun lovers; an east window for plants that like to be cool but need little light, such as ferns; a west window for plants that need medium light. Of course, in winter months a south window is suitable for all plants, because light intensities are much lower than in summer. Plants should be stood in a tray of pebbles and water

(with the water reaching only to the top of the stones) and should be misted twice a day, especially in winter. When you put the plant in as bright a spot as possible, you are helping to make the change in the light conditions less dramatic; the tray of stones and water, along with the misting, makes the sudden drop in humidity less damaging. Because we are lucky enough to have central heating, the temperature factor need not be considered.

As well as acclimatizing and caring for your new plants, you must also consider all the plants you already have. The number of times I have gone to see people whose prize plant, which they have had for years, has suddenly contracted bugs! Nearly all these plants, which had enjoyed perfect health until that moment, had picked up bugs from a new arrival. So move all your existing plants at least three feet away from their new companion. As you are misting and watering, keep a sharp eye out for those nasty horrible beasties!

After three or four weeks of quarantine and adjustment, your new plant should be ready to move to its own special spot. Check it over once more very closely; if you are satisfied that it's pest free, then you may arrange it among your other plants.

I know this all sounds very time consuming and complicated, but it really is quite simple and takes very little time at all. If you have a permanent spot for new arrivals, your job is simplified even more.

3

Getting to Know You

Now that you have successfully acquired a healthy new plant, your next job is to keep it looking beautiful. In this chapter, as I promised, I'm afraid I'm going to get very boring and technical in my description of all the tiny details of care necessary to keep your plant going strong, so let's break the chapter into three parts: light, water, and general care.

Regardless of whether I say 2 cups, or 5 feet, or once a week, I don't want you to dole out your plant care like an exacting scientist: 'Right, it is three o'clock and time for their 30 centimetres of water.' In no circumstances do I want you to act like that. Instead, in the same way that your grandmother baked first-rate cakes, never once using a measuring spoon, you will grow lovely plants without using a measuring cup or a light meter. In caring for plants, the best indoor gardener is always the one who, when faced with a decision or problem, does nothing more than use Common Sense. That last sentence is the most important in this chapter, if not in this book, and now that I have armed you with this knowledge I will make your common sense deductions a little easier by providing you with the facts.

This SANSEVIERIA thrives at a North-facing window

Light

There are two important factors to be considered when you are trying to decide where to put your plant so that it gets the right amount of light. The first is to know how much light your particular plant needs, for all house plants require different intensities. Don't assume that if your 'X' is doing well in a certain spot, your new 'Y' will, too. As I mentioned earlier, you should always identify any new plant in a plant book, noting the amount of light your plant requires: direct sunlight, bright diffused light, moderate to fair light, or low light.

I realize that if you know your new plant must have moderate light, that won't help unless you know exactly what moderate light means. Now if everyone owned a light meter with foot-candle readings, my job would be simple. Unfortunately, everyone doesn't, so I shall have to resort to charts. And that brings me to the second point: you must decide how much light your plant will receive in the place where you want to put it. In our country, the brightest possible light in your home is to be found at a south-facing window. A very large south window, unobstructed, can safely light a plant needing only low light up to 20 feet away from it. But let's not get all excited and start placing all your low-light lovers 20 feet from your south window—there are many things to consider before you decide on the actual strength of the light there.

Here is a check list for later reference:

A In which direction is my window facing?

B How large is it?

C Is it obstructed in any way?

D Is the plant in line with the window? (. . . not behind a curtain or shielded by the wall beside the window, I mean.)

E How far away from the window will the plant be?

Now to explain each one:

A Direction

Southern light is the strongest; there's not much to choose between east and west windows—each provides moderate (medium) light; light from the north is considered low in intensity. Perhaps your source of light is from above—a skylight or court with a glass roof—or you have a sunroom or a room that is mostly glass. If so, the light let in is always excellent. To gauge from the chart exactly how much light can be expected from these sources, treat them all as large, south-facing windows.

. . . perhaps you have a sunroom

B   Size

The size of a window affects the intensity of light, regardless of which direction the window is facing. Let's imagine that there are only three sizes of windows (large, medium, and small) instead of the thousand-and-one sizes there really are. A window over 7 to 8 feet wide by 4 to 5 feet deep may be considered large; one that measures approximately 3 to 4 feet wide by 4 to 5 feet deep is a medium window, and a small one would be 2 to 3 feet or less in either width or height. My reason for mentioning these sizes is not to make sure you use a tape measure, but to help you decide which category your window falls into on the chart.

C   Obstructions

A large south-facing window that looks out onto a brick wall is not going to be a very good source of light! An unobstructed window has nothing beside, above, or in front of it to block out the sun. If there aren't any buildings or trees, how about overhangs from the roof or balconies? An overhang more than 3 feet deep means the window is obstructed. Then there is the perfect view out and up—but with towering structures on both sides that cut out hours of sun. When you are checking a window on the chart, any object that may block out even a few hours of sun is to be considered an obstruction.

D   Angle of Light

Light travels in a straight line, therefore you must keep your plant within the line of light entering from the window. Be sure your plant isn't standing in shadow. A plant placed in the corner will only receive reflected light from the floor, walls, and ceiling—light very definitely not strong enough to support many kinds of plants.

E Distance

The further away from a light source you are, the weaker the light will be. To decide how far away from the window you may place your plant, take the four previous points in the check list into consideration and keep in mind the light specifications for your plant.

A note about drapes and sheers: The first thing an indoor gardener should do each morning is to open all drapes and sheers at any window that is supplying a plant with light. Sheers reduce the strength of light by about half; if you cannot pull them back because the rugs may fade or the furniture warp, cut in half any information given to you on the chart, no matter what direction the window faces.

As an example of how to use the chart, let's say the plant you bought was an English Ivy (*Hedera helix*), and in check-

WINDOW		DIRECTION											
SIZE	TYPE	SOUTH				EAST / WEST				NORTH			
"LARGE"	OBSTRUCTED												
	UNOBS.												
"MEDIUM"	OBSTRUCTED												
	UNOBS.												
"SMALL"	OBSTRUCTED												
	UNOBS.												
DISTANCE AWAY IN FEET ⟶		1 TO 3	4 TO 6	7 TO 9	10 TO 12	1 TO 3	4 TO 6	7 TO 9	10 TO 12	1 TO 3	4 TO 6	7 TO 9	10 TO 12

LEGEND: ‖ BRIGHT /// MODERATE ⊠ FAIR ■ INSUFFICIENT

WINDOW – LIGHT CHART

ing the book you found that its light requirements were 'bright indirect to open shade'. You would like the ivy to reside on the buffet in the dining room. You see that the dining-room window faces east, is medium sized, unobstructed, and that the position you have chosen on the buffet is 7 feet from the window. Look at the chart. Find the medium window, unobstructed column. Move to the east/west section. Look at the distance: your spot is 7 feet away, so you would check the 5-10 feet box in the east/west section of the Medium Unobstructed Window column, finding crossed diagonal lines which signify fair light. Obviously the spot will be suitable.

The day may come when you buy a plant that you can't identify, therefore you won't know just how much light it needs. Should that happen, these suggestions may help you:

A   Plants with two-coloured leaves *usually* need direct or bright to indirect light. (By 'two-coloured leaves' I mean basic green plus white, red, yellow, or purple areas in any variety of markings.)

B   Most cacti (succulents) need bright direct light or sunlight.

C   Most plants with large dark-green leaves prefer medium or indirect light, or will do well in low light—that is, *adequate* light.

D   Plants that flower, especially those that are in flower, usually need *bright* direct or indirect light.

E   Most vines and creepers do well in moderate to fair light or in low light.

F   Most tree-like large plants require bright indirect light.

G   Most semi-succulents (plants with fat, fleshy leaves) require bright or indirect light, or occasional sun.

In the preceding tips, I made liberal use of the words 'most' and 'usually' in each statement, simply because, in dealing with plant care, whenever one tries to state an absolute, one or two species always march forward to disprove one's absolute. Therefore, to check that you aren't trying to grow a breaker of all rules, remember to watch the new growth and leaves of your plant after it has been placed, to see whether or not it is reacting properly to the light. When a plant is properly lighted, it will continue to grow in much the same way as it did before you bought it.

In my experience, I have only very occasionally found plants suffering from too much light, but if you happen to have an incredibly large south-facing window or live in a glass palace, it's entirely possible! One of the symptoms is that the leaf colour, either all over or on the edges, becomes weakened or bleached, and changes to a very pale greenish yellow, white, or orange. Sometimes plants actually seem to have been burned by the hot sunlight: the topmost leaves facing the light turn crisp and brown in large patches as the scorched cells dry up. Some plants try to escape the strong light by curling up or wilting as if they were too dry, even though the soil may be quite moist.

At the opposite extreme, too little light is one of the major causes of plant troubles; it makes *life* difficult for any plant, let alone growth. If there is too little light, any new growth is puny, small, and pale in colour. In an attempt to reach the light, the length of the stems increases unbelievably, resulting in long, leggy-looking plants which bear little resemblance to the original—in fact, in very advanced stages of this condition, some plants are almost impossible to identify. Multicoloured plants, and plants with variegated leaves, begin to produce only ordinary green leaves. Bushy plants will lose their bottom and inside leaves, ultimately retaining only the top and outside growth that's 'all right, but nothing to look at,' according to the disappointed owner. Leaves may bend to catch light, and will retain these ugly and unnatural shapes. New growth on plants that once had rough, textured leaves becomes smooth and shiny; plants that should have natural hairy leaves will grow bald ones.

27

Water

'How much water should I give my ...?' This is the most frequently asked of all the questions I come across in my job as plant doctor. Regardless of the type of plant my client has, or how much water it might require, on every occasion I stress one particular point: *Always feel the soil before rewatering.* If you feel the soil of your house plants every two or three days, you can keep yourself well informed about their watering needs. As with light, the need for water varies from one plant to the next; correct identification of your plant helps you to give it approximately the right amount. Most books divide plants into three basic groups: those that like to stay on the dry side, those that should dry out to a certain extent between waterings, and those that like to stay constantly and evenly damp or moist. When you have arrived at the statement that best applies to your plant, it's again time to don your detective outfit and to begin making crafty deductions.

'What size of pot is my plant in, and how much water does it need?' I have often chuckled to myself when I have seen or heard of someone being given a specific amount of water as the correct amount for, let's say, a plant that likes to stay moist. 'Give it a cup and a half once a week,' for instance. Hearing that, I always picture two things: a somewhat frustrated person trying to get 1½ cups of water into a thimble-sized pot, and another confidently pouring 1½ cups into a pot the size of a modest swimming pool. To help you decide how much water to use when watering becomes necessary, here is a list of pot sizes (diameters) and approximate amounts.

6 – 10″	½ – ¾ cup
10 – 12″	¾ – 1 cup
12 – 16″	1 – 2 cups
16 – 18″	2 – 3 cups
18 – 21″	3 cups – 1 quart

Unless the pot is vast in size, giving the occupant more than 1 to 1½ quarts of water at a time is very dangerous; instead, give smaller amounts more often.

'How often should I water my plant?' If the soil for a plant that needs to stay moist feels dry to your touch on the surface only, then it's time to rewater—but only enough to moisten the soil. For a plant that must be dry, you should keep the soil dry to a point deep down in the pot—but how deep? How much water the plant itself needs, and the size of the pot, determine the correct depth to which you should allow the soil to be dry, and, of course, when I talk about depth of dryness, I mean how deep you can put your finger into the soil before feeling the coolness of moisture. I know that by now you must be wondering why I am carrying on and on about the depth of dryness. If I thought I could give you even a reasonable length of time to wait between waterings, I would, but it can't be done. It can't be done because the conditions in all our homes are different, the types of soil used vary too greatly, and the influences of the seasons can *all* cause the soil in your plant's pot to dry at different rates. To repeat: if you feel the soil frequently, you will never over- or under-water any of your plants.

To make your job easier, I have drawn up another chart. At the side I have given the diameters of the pot; across the top, the amounts of moisture plants are likely to need, grouped into three basic types. The information between these reference points gives you the maximum and minimum depths to which the soil should be allowed to dry between each watering.

Before I go on, I must mention the shallow pot and the pot without a drainage hole. In both my watering charts I have assumed that, as the diameter of the pot increases in size, so too does the depth of the pot—if it is the standard flowerpot shape. But sometimes, to create a particular effect, a pot or planter will be broad but shallow. If you have a pot 18 inches in diameter and only 3 inches deep, you will, of course, have to adjust the amount of water and the length of

POT DIAMETER	SOIL MOISTURE:		
	DRY	AVERAGE	EVENLY MOIST
under 6"	DIRECTIONS SAME FOR ALL SIZES: ↓	$\frac{1}{4}$ TO $\frac{1}{2}$ "	ALLOW SURFACE ONLY TO DRY....
6~10"	AT LEAST HALF-WAY INTO THE POT.... TO COMPLETELY DRY.... Then RE-WATER.	$\frac{1}{2}$ TO $\frac{3}{4}$ "	SURFACE TO $\frac{1}{4}$ "
10~12"		$\frac{3}{4}$ TO 1 "	$\frac{1}{4}$ TO $\frac{1}{2}$ "
12-16"		1 TO $1\frac{1}{2}$ "	$\frac{1}{2}$ TO $\frac{3}{4}$ "
16~18"		$1\frac{1}{2}$ TO $2\frac{1}{2}$ "	$\frac{3}{4}$ TO 1 "
18-21"		$2\frac{1}{2}$ TO $3\frac{1}{2}$ "	1 TO 2 "
over 21"		$3\frac{1}{2}$ " TO $\frac{1}{4}$ OF DEPTH OF POT	2" TO $\frac{1}{8}$ OF DEPTH OF POT

CHART for DEPTHS of SOIL DRYNESS

time between waterings, using the method of trial and (though I hope not) error. Certain plants thrive in very well-drained soil, where the water runs swiftly to the bottom of the pot. In a pot without a drainage hole or in a solid fiberglas planter, some water buildup that your finger cannot feel may occur even after the normal drying-out procedure, and it's best to tip all pots that lack drainage on their sides at least once a month to see whether they still hold sufficient water to make rewatering unnecessary.

If you have been unable to identify an unusual new plant, you will again be forced to decide for yourself how much water it needs. It's safest to treat the new plant as one that needs moderate watering, watching it carefully for signs of over- or under-watering.

If your plant is being over-watered:

1 the leaves turn yellow, brown, or black, and are too supple or soggy

2 any new growth may rot and fall off

3 the stems of the plant become soft and yellow or spotted with black

4 the whole plant may wilt, even though the soil is still moist

5 the roots will look and smell rotten

6 the leaves may fall off when they are still green, even though the light is right

If your plant is being under-watered:

1 the leaf-tips and edges turn brown or yellow, becoming crisp and dry

2 the leaves fade; the areas between the veins turn a pale green or yellow

3 new leaves won't uncurl or reach maturity

4 the plant wilts frequently

5 the roots are brittle and dry

6 the stalks sometimes wrinkle and shrink in size

Lastly, all plants should be watered with water at room temperature. The best way to have a supply of this available when you need it is to keep a gallon or two standing ready at all times. Whenever you use some, fill the tub up again. You see, in nature, the rain that falls on plants is at approximately the same temperature as the air surrounding them. If a plant growing in 20°C soil is watered with 2°C water, the chill can be a shock to its delicate system; if the plant is particularly sensitive, a shock like that can be disastrous. And there's another benefit from letting the water for watering stand for a while before you use it. In most cities the water is chlorinated—sometimes it even smells of bleach. Chlorine is not good for plants, but it can easily be removed if you let the water stand for 24 hours in an open, wide-necked container—by that time the chlorine will have completely evaporated. Other additives are the salts that can be put in to make water 'soft'; try to use a tap that is not connected to a soft-water system, for the salts are also harmful to plants.

General Care

Turning   Plants like to take full advantage of the light. When a plant is placed next to a window, it will begin to turn its leaves towards the sun. When it produces new growth, that too will grow towards the sun, and the result will be a one-sided plant that is quite hideous. I'm sure we've all seen those poor neglected things in old barbershops or restaurants, their leaves pressed up against the glass. Once you are inside one of these establishments, all you see of the plant are its pot, stems, and shadow. To rectify this problem, turn all your plants about a quarter of the way round once a week. This rotation forces the leaves to keep turning to the light, and will give you a symmetrical plant that looks healthy from all directions.

Rotating   For the sake of good design it is sometimes necessary to set plants in spots where they are not getting quite enough light. If you do this, you should only use plants that don't mind low light anyway. Once you have put a plant in an area that is inadequately lit, I suggest you let it take turns with another plant once every two weeks to a month; in other words, give the plant that is in poor light a 'vacation' in a better-lit place every two weeks. You should have another low-light plant to switch with it, so that the poorly lit spot will have a happy, healthy plant in it all the time.

Pinching   Pinching out new growth is a method usually used on vines and creepers, but it can be practised on all plants. When you pinch your plant, you force it to branch out, and if you are dedicated enough, you can virtually change it to any shape you wish. Let's say you have a Grape Ivy that has five main stems or branches, and that they are getting longer and more gangly by the day. Its little niche is already cramped, and you would like your ivy to become thicker, not larger. Simply pinch off the growing points on each of the long branches, and every time you water the plant have another look at those branches. If Ivy has tried to produce another leaf-bud at the end again, relentlessly pinch it out! At first most plants are quite stubborn—they keep on doing exactly what *they* want to do; but if you are stern, the plant will eventually give in to your determination and will branch out from other, more desirable places. Pinching is definitely an Art.

Atomizing (Misting)   It is a godsend to plants to have their leaves sprayed with water at room temperature once a day. Misting provides additional moisture and helps to remove dust. A conscientious indoor gardener should start or end each day with atomizer in hand. Misting your plants can be very relaxing, and is an invaluable way of really getting to know your plants.

Cleaning   Two or three times a year it will become necessary to get down to the drudgery of cleaning your house plants. Though it may be growing beautifully for you, a dusty Schefflera is a sorry sight indeed. The best cleaning equipment is a slightly damp, soft cloth. Put your hand, palm upwards, under the leaf and draw the cloth outwards to the leaf tip. I've found it's unwise to try to clean a leaf by stroking back and forth because, when the cloth is being pushed in towards the base of the leaf, the leaf usually buckles; nine times out of ten it cracks where it was bent, and another good leaf is lost. Be very gentle—and clean the tops of the leaves only, not the undersides.

For some strange reason, one that escapes me entirely, certain people like to shine their plants in the same way as they would their silver or floors. A high-gloss Philodendron, flashing light from every angle like a multi-faceted diamond, absolutely offends me! The artificial-looking green object has so many coats of leaf shine that you could comb your hair in its reflection. In addition to making your plants look like genuine plastic, excessive use of any leaf-shining product is not good for them. The leaves are covered with tiny holes (pores) for breathing and for releasing excess water. Two or three coats of leaf shine, mixed with the dust that was trapped as it was sprayed on, can block these little holes. When most of the holes are blocked, the death of the leaf is not far off. If you absolutely must shine your plants, use milk. The butterfat in the milk will remain on the leaf, giving it a soft glow. To shine your plant with milk, clean your plant as I have described, using a mixture of milk and water (to cut down on the butterfat) instead of milk alone.

milk, water, and soft cloth

4

Suddenly ...

I went to visit a friend of mine a few weeks ago. She lives in a beautiful 1930ish house with large rooms, a sunroom, and dark wood panelling throughout, overlooking a large park. Six months ago, when she married and moved with her husband into this house, their new home, they received a number of house plants as combined housewarming and wedding gifts. At that time I had helped my friends to place their plants in the best growing spots, and had written out a care sheet setting out the correct watering for each of their green friends.

Before sitting down in the living room, I glanced around the room, as I usually do, taking in the condition of each plant as I saw it. One of the plants, a *Podocarpus macrophylla* (African Pine) stood in a corner next to the window, obviously quite dead. When a Podocarpus dies, it usually simply dries out, almost unnoticeably, turning a grey-green colour but without losing a single leaf. True to form, theirs had done just that.

Still looking at the remains, I said, 'Your Podocarpus sure is doing nicely!' thinking that my friend knew the poor thing had died. 'Oh thank you,' she beamed. 'Yes, it is doing well, isn't it? You know, it hasn't lost a leaf.' I laughed and

replied, 'Dead, but hasn't lost a leaf; that *is* good.' A puzzled expression crossed her face, as she said, 'It's not dead, it's only dusty.' So I picked a few brittle leaves, showed them to her, and thought I had convinced her that the plant was indeed dead.

And then a week later I went to visit her again. Apparently she and her husband had discussed with each other exactly what condition their Podocarpus really was in, and by the time I arrived they had concluded that the plant was definitely *not* dead—because it had looked like that for months and they had been watering it regularly. The reason for their certainty was simple: every time they went to rewater it, they saw that the soil had dried out. Obviously the water had to be going somewhere, therefore there was no question in their minds that the plant was drinking heartily. (It hadn't occurred to them that the dry air in the room might be doing exactly the same thing.) I guess that their strong sentimental attachment to their Podocarpus stood in the way of cold logic. As for what had gone wrong, it was unfortunately too late to find out.

There may come a day when you, too, will have a plant that is starting to die, but unlike my confident friends in the story I hope that you will be watching it a little more carefully, will notice as soon as it's not up to par, and do something before it's too late. It isn't luck that gives some people green thumbs, it's what they do *right*, when they are confronted with a problem plant, that enables them to get through the crisis with flying colours. I'm asking you to become very intimately acquainted with your plants: whenever you are watering, misting, or turning them, give them a quick going over to see if they are still healthy.

Though it's a sad occasion, I love to be confronted with an ailing plant. I have to decide exactly what is wrong by asking my client many questions as well as carefully checking the plant over. When you feel ill and visit the doctor, he doesn't just take a quick glance at you and immediately tell you what is wrong; he asks you questions, runs tests, and feels the spot that hurts—not until then does he make his decision and begin treatment. When you are being your own plant doctor, you should do the same: investigate, draw a conclusion, then act on it immediately.

To start a campaign to revive an ailing plant, remove any dead or dying leaves or stems, inspecting the core of a piece of dead stem for possible signs of rot, and noting the feel and look of the areas you suspect. Once you have removed all the damage, the plant looks better, and you will find it easier to tell whether or not you have diagnosed the problem correctly. If the plant doesn't grow any more short-lived leaves after the surgery and treatment, or fewer of them appear, you have probably identified the plant's ailment correctly. But if sickly leaves continue to show with the same regularity, you must investigate still further. I have often found a client's plant to be suffering from more than one malady at the same time—so if you feel that possible mistakes in care have been rectified, but the plant still seems to be dying, perhaps something else has been bothering it all along. Sometimes, in addition to the more obvious problems that can beset a plant, it may suddenly start to look unhealthy even when all the rules of plant care are being properly followed. If this happens, try to think of anything that may have occurred recently to cause the trouble.

Some months ago I visited a sick Benjamina. My client had owned it for three years and, until a few days before I was asked to come, it had positively thrived. She was watering it correctly, it was in good light, had no bugs, and had not been through a drastic change in temperature, yet it was definitely giving up. After carefully checking over the plant, I began to ask questions. We finally arrived at the answer. A few weeks earlier, her old atomizer had broken. Before hurrying out to buy a new one, she remembered that she had a perfectly good one: a container and applicator of a bathroom and kitchen cleanser. She dumped out the dregs, filled it with water, and misted her Benjamina with it. A few days later the leaves began to fall. A chemical in that cleanser didn't agree with Benjaminas!

When one or two leaves turn yellow on a plant, especially a large one, it's not always an indication that something is wrong. There are a number of plants, such as the long-stalked ones, that naturally lose their lower leaves. If you have a plant that loses a few of them each month but is otherwise doing well, don't worry about it. Most members of the Dracaena family, for example, only hold on to about 3 feet of growth at the top of a long stalk, even when they are in a greenhouse. I have often been called to a client's house because a particularly special plant was 'dying', only to find out that the unhappy owner possessed a healthy plant doing exactly what it was supposed to. Someone once phoned me in an absolute dither: her 6-foot Peruvian cactus, which she had had for a year, was developing a cancerous disease. She imagined any apparently unusual and unattractive growths to be malignant, and was sure the end result was to be the death of her favourite plant. The fact that I must come immediately was obvious; failing to calm her over the telephone, I made a house call the same evening. The growths of her Peruvian cactus were not colonies of horrible bugs, cancerous tumours, or ever-swelling moulds or fungi, but were instead the buds of flowers, which later graced her home with their soft creamy colour and large floppy petals.

Emergency Department

The Fallen Plant   Crash! Bowser has been clumsy again. But this time, instead of your cherished Dresden figurine, it was your Columnea that was just about to bloom. After pronouncing Bowser persona non grata and banishing him to the backyard, what should you do with the mess that was your Columnea? Getting it into another pot quickly ought to be your first concern, but cover and moisten the root ball before you run to the store. If some of the roots have been badly damaged, be very careful, when repotting, not to disturb the ones that are intact. Don't tamp the soil down; instead, sprinkle it in until the pot is full, then tap the pot against a solid object to further settle it. Add more soil, then water liberally. If there are damaged branches, cut them off at the break and try to root them in water, moist peat moss, or sandy soil. If your plant was healthy before its fall, it will, even though quite crushed, start to grow again energetically. You may even end up with two or three plants in place of one.

The Polluted Plant   If you are doing any major redecorating, painting, or other similar work at home, it is always

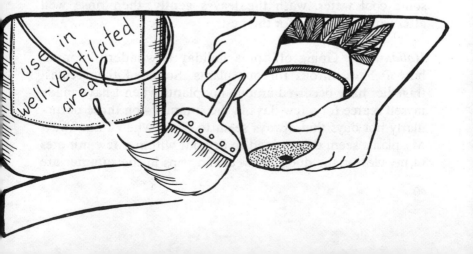

wise to keep your plants out of the areas where the action is. Apart from accidental damage caused by overzealous workmen, and the thick dust that settles, stifling your plants and blocking out light, there is a third danger to consider. Plumbers, painters, and carpenters use a number of chemical aids to perform their tasks, and any one of these paints or glues, for example, contains chemicals which, when released into the air, could cause cell damage, leaf drop, and possible death. If your plant shows some signs of distress the day after that big can of smelly stuff was used to clean out the backed-up drain, you can probably blame the trouble on whatever was in the air. Move the plants to a part of your dwelling where the smell isn't so noticeable, and mist them until they drip to flush away any sediment that might be adhering to the leaves.

As far as pollution is concerned, possible damage to our house plants is no worse than the damage to ourselves. If they begin to decline and you feel sure the real cause is the polluted atmosphere, whatever is killing them is certainly not good for you, either. Staying upset is the best remedy: do something to stop the polluter!

Whenever you are waging war against flies, hornets, or other household pests, don't spray near your plants—especially not on them. Some pesticides, in particular the oil-based ones, are harmful to delicate foliage. Always move plants away from the area you are about to fumigate. If you do accidentally spray a plant, add a few mild soap flakes to some cool water, wash the leaves gently, then rinse well afterwards and hope for the best.

Holidays   Going off for a holiday is wonderful for us, but often disastrous for our plants. Some of the greatest tragedies have occurred among my plants when I have made myself scarce for a few days in the summer—on those particularly hot days that always seem to come when I am away. My plants seem determined to dry out within a few minutes of my closing the door. So weekend trips in the summer are

40

the most dangerous of all. For two or three days your little home is locked up, no fresh air or life-saving mist, perhaps not even any air conditioning, drapes drawn shut—the atmosphere inside becomes oppressive. And the plants wilt almost immediately. Returning from your weekend of fun and relaxation, you are greeted with a scene of devastation comparable to a dust storm in the Sahara. It never seems to be the large plants that are bothered by the few days of agony, but the little guys in small pots, who dry out at a rate faster than a speeding bullet.

Prevention is always the best cure. If you are off for a few days, all your plants should be well watered before you leave, and the smaller pots, especially the earthenware ones, should be stood in water. Every home has a ready-made anti-death device: a handy item called a bathtub. Gather up all your small plants, also any large ones in the habit of drying up quickly, and place the whole lot in the bathtub in an inch or so of water. Now you can leave with a carefree, confident air—but for no more than two or three days. Don't expect your plants to enjoy living for a week in the tub, for conditions could rapidly come to resemble those of a gloomy swamp. If you are leaving for more than four days, a friend or relative should be comandeered to serve your cause.

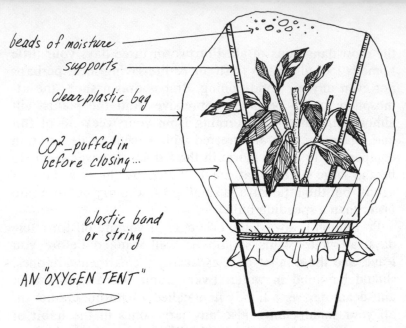

beads of moisture

supports

clear plastic bag

CO_2-puffed in before closing...

elastic band or string

AN "OXYGEN TENT"

What to do if you didn't take preventive measures? Remove any brown and dead leaves, then thoroughly drench and mist all your plants. The next day you may feel relieved when most of them have rallied. As for the ones that haven't, there is a last hope. The assumed spark of life must be fanned—in an 'oxygen tent'. Put a large clear plastic bag over the semi-deceased victim, propping it up with sticks or knitting needles if necessary. Have ready an elastic band that will fit snugly around the rim of the pot to hold the open end of the bag in tight. Before you seal off this little environment, use your atomizer to spray mist into it, and puff it out with a good lungful of carbon dioxide. Place the plant in medium light and check it often. If new growth does not begin within three or four weeks, say a short prayer, reflect on the causes of the fatality, and vow that your plant will not have died in vain.

The main problem a long winter trip could cause is that your plants may freeze or suffer from acute cold while you are away, but this is unlikely unless your furnace chronically breaks down, or you are trying to save many pennies on the heating bill during your absence. If you live in an apartment, there should be no problem with the cold at all. Nevertheless, no matter where you live, there are precautions you should take. When you are away, never leave a window open in the room where the plants are—a blizzard or record cold may strike. Don't leave plants on a window ledge and pull the drapes shut behind them. The drapes act as an insulator, preventing the warmth of the room from reaching the window. After a plant has been subjected to extremely low temperatures, its only hope for possible recovery is again the misted, warm treatment in the clear plastic bag. A frozen plant is usually very difficult to revive, so if nothing good happens after those three to four weeks, put on a black armband and play taps. You tried.

The final problem that can occur while you are on a holiday is, I'm afraid, caused by the well-meaning friend or relative who has devotedly over-watered your plants. Try not to throw a tantrum, but calmly drain off the excess water, check for water build-up in solid-bottom planters, and patiently wait for your plants to dry out. Then give them slightly less water than usual for about a month. The drying of the soil and root ball stimulates root growth and ultimately strengthens the plant.

You may come across a plant that has suffered an injustice (never mind how), has lost all its leaves, and looks for all the world dead. As I mentioned earlier, I have an apartment full of plants that were pronounced dead by defeated clients and friends before they were passed on to me, and that have lived to flourish and bloom again. Don't give up in despair when a plant has become even much less than perfect. Check for signs of life: green stems or trunk with the sap still running (break off a piece of stem to see); undamaged, fresh-smelling roots; a layer of green under a bark-covered stem (scratch the stem and look); a tiny shoot at the crown. If you spot any of these encouraging signs, get out the plastic intensive-care unit, and devote more time and attention to that particular plant. Remember, if you honestly like house plants, you won't give up on any of them.

5

Those Nasty
Horrible Beasties

*Caution: Do not use any of the sprays I mention
without first carefully reading the label on the container, and noting which types of plants it cannot be
used on. Also, before spraying, read the section
called* **Using Pesticides** *later in this chapter.*

Gloomy is the day you are watering your plants and realize
one of them has bugs! A metamorphosis should occur,
changing you from a gentle, peace-loving individual into a
ruthless Commander, waging war against the enemies with
only one thought in mind: complete and total destruction of
their entire population. Resist the impulse to grab the infected plant and throw it out of the house. No, don't give up
so easily; fight for what is yours—better still, fight for the
life of your poor defenceless plant, who relies on you for
everything.

Another good line of propaganda, strong enough I hope
to interest you in battling the bugs: whenever you do detect
these little horrors on your plant, it is imperative that you
quarantine not only that particular plant but inspect all your
others to make sure that they have not been infected by the

patient. Keep him at least 10 feet away from his nearest companion, in sufficient light, until you are certain that the bugs have all gone.

To deal with pests effectively, you must know what kind they are; certain insecticides may be ineffective against one sort of bug, but deadly to the species they are designed to combat. To help you decide which bugs are vindictively attacking you and yours, I have made a list of the most famous ones, what they look like, what kind of damage they do, what telltale signs they leave behind them, and how to prevent them and cure their victims.

Spider Mites, alias Red Spiders

When some of my clients find they are sharing their living quarters with red spiders, they immediately start to feel itchy. This urge to scratch is purely psychological; none of the little creepy crawlers that munch on greenery have the urge to eat people.

I could probably write more than one chapter on the activities of spider mites—there seem to be few plants they don't think are tasty and delicious; most of them they just love, and probably every plant you own is a potential supper for red spiders, so watch out. A spider mite is *small*. Even a big, muscle-bound red spider is under $^1/_{16}"$ across, so don't expect to see great red dots roving over your plant. For that matter, don't expect them to be red, because mites (of which the red spider is one) come in all colours. The best way to find them is with a magnifying glass. If you don't have one handy, then check the damage to the plant and the deposits on the leaves.

A mature leaf that has mites on it shows many signs that the bugs are trying to wipe it out. In the early stages of infestation, the leaf stays a natural colour (bright green, for instance) all over, except for tiny white dots on the under-side that look like a sprinkle of salt. The dots are semitransparent, and are either discarded mite-skins or the actual mite (sometimes two tiny black 'eye' spots may be detected, dodging out of the way of your finger). As the bugs make themselves at home, the leaf becomes pale on top, with pinpoint-sized, transparent, chewed-away areas of cells, and the underside will begin to turn a rusty colour. In the advanced stages, when the leaf is all but dead, the underside shows the rusty colour of many red spiders, shiny secretions, and the gritty remains of shed skins; the bugs spin thread-like webs across any open areas that hinder the direct route to juicier feeding grounds. But I hope you will never allow any of your plants to reach this stage. Another sign of spider mites is deformed new growth. As a new little leaf appears, some spider mites climb up onto it to enjoy a fresher, more tender salad; small areas of the leaf are killed off, and the rest of it expands as it grows, the dead areas causing the leaf to buckle like a crumpled piece of tinfoil. Mites reproduce with lightning speed, so once they are discovered they should be dealt with immediately.

The only effective method of removing red spiders is a repeated course of spraying with a pesticide that claims to be effective against them, but see the short paragraph headed *Caution* at the beginning of this chapter. Just spraying once will not do the job: even if you killed every last living mite on the plant in one drenching (which is unlikely), in a short time more eggs would hatch and you would be back where you started. I've found that the best campaign is to spray the plant once a week for four weeks, then once every two weeks. After the sixth treatment, check the plant for any signs of renewed activity. A systemic spray is best, because the spray enters the plant as well as staying on the foliage, and the plant itself becomes poisonous to red spider. There are a number of systemic sprays on the market; use any which claim to bring mites under control. If you own a particularly delicate plant and you are afraid it may be allergic to systemics, your next choice might be an oil spray; but remember that oil sprays should never be used on cacti.

Other pesticides effective against red spiders are those containing either diazinon or malathion. It is advisable to test the pesticide on a small area, before you go all out, to judge the plant's tolerance to the pesticide. You can help the chemical discouragers do their job by thoroughly washing the whole plant—leaves, stems, and all—before each spraying session. And mites don't like to be misted. Heavy misting every day, concentrating on the undersides of the leaves, also makes life difficult for our squatter the red spider!

Mealybugs

These insects can be seen with the naked eye. They are brownish or greyish-white, and cover themselves with a fuzzy, cottony substance for protection. The plant appears to have fluffy spots and dots along the stems, in the joints of the branches, clustered on the undersides of leaves, under the sheaths of its bark, or, if it is a cactus, nestled between the prickles—usually at the top of the plant. Mealybugs slowly kill the plant by sucking its juices and starving it to death. Symptons of mealybug attacks are: leaves that turn pale or brown and then drop off; stunted, weak, or dried-out new growth; dry patches on the leaves; and drooping branches. Luckily, mealybugs are not difficult to get rid of—spraying once every two weeks for six or eight weeks does the trick (see the *Caution* at the beginning of this chapter). Use any spray that guarantees to kill mealybugs; the systemic ones are best, because, if the cottony coverings around the bugs are not thoroughly drenched, the pesticide may not penetrate to the bug, and he will be left to continue his life as if nothing had happened. Be sure to get the pesticide down into all the nooks and crannies the plant may have, for there will surely be one or two of these little aggravations hiding there, waiting for you to finish spraying. It is advisable to wash any visible mealybugs off the infected plant between sprayings, or you might use mild soap and water to wipe them off. Rubbing alcohol may be used as an effective *temporary* measure, but I suggest you only use it if other remedies are not available, for I've found that it often damages the plant, causing dried, withered leaves.

Scale

Scale insects come in four colours—white, black, tan, or brown. Shaped like little plates or discs, scale cling to the trunks, branches, stems, veins, and leaves of the plant, sucking the sap of their unfortunate host. Scale are fairly large when fully developed (the adults are hard little lumps about ⅛" across) and easily seen on your plant; in fact you might even feel brave enough to pick them off—not a difficult job because only the young move, the adults remain in the same spot. Like mealybugs, scale cause the leaves to drop and new growth to become stunted, and a general overall sickly look. In advanced infestations, the plant will become covered with a sticky, shiny film which blocks the leaf pores. Wash this film off thoroughly with soap (real soap or soap flakes, not detergent) and water, then spray with either diazinon, or a systemic pesticide, or an oil spray. But don't begin to spray without reading the *Caution* at the beginning of this chapter. Wash and spray the plant at least four times: once every three weeks. Then watch often for the return of the pests. Again like mealybugs, scale enjoy wedging themselves into small cracks or crevices and between stems and stalks. Be sure not to miss these places—douse them well.

White Fly

White flies make particular nuisances of themselves, for the simple reason that they can fly, which makes the quarantine period rather difficult both for plants and their owners. Fuchsia, tomatoes, lantana, and Jerusalem cherries seem to

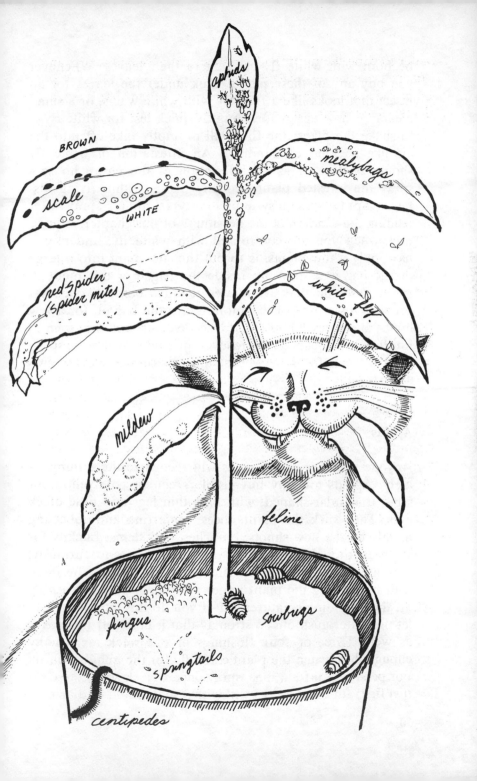

be born with white fly clinging to their leaves. Whenever you buy any of these plants, look under the leaves for an insect that looks like a fruit fly with white wings, or a small creamy-yellow egg-shaped bug. A quick test for white fly is to shake the plant; the flies will promptly take off into the air like a cloud of dandruff. An infestation of white fly should be treated as an infestation of the entire house — spray the infested plant and any plants within flying distance. Spray with a systemic spray or an oil spray after reading the *Caution* at the beginning of this chapter. A good trick when you are confronted with white fly, and if you have only a few plants, is to put the sick plant into a large plastic bag and spray up inside the bag. For this method, use a pesticide that evaporates readily — perhaps one that contains malathion or diazinon. Leave the bag on for a few hours, and spray a household insecticide around the room to finish off the escapees. Whichever method you choose, spray once a week for four weeks, then twice more every two weeks.

Aphids

Anyone who has grown roses will recognize these immediately. Aphids are tiny but visible green or pale-yellow insects, triangular-shaped, with long thin legs and little black eyes. They suck the plant juices, preferring and collecting mainly on the new shoots, branches, and stems. Luckily for us, even though these bugs reproduce fast and furiously, they are easily got rid of. Minor infestations can be dealt with by holding the plant under a tap or hose and washing off the offending creatures, but if you do this, be sure not to let the water gush out so strongly that it takes off the leaves as well. Three or four flushings in one week are usually enough, but watch the plant carefully for the aphids' return. For persistent infestations, spray once a week (read the *Caution* first) for three weeks with either malathion, or diazinon, or a systemic spray. The soft bodies of the aphids make them easy prey for your atomizer of pesticide.

Crawlers and Soil Beasties

Millipedes, centipedes, ants, roaches, silverfish, and soil dwellers such as springtails, sowbugs or carpenter bugs, and fungus gnats must all be dealt with by treating not the plant but either the soil and pot or the room itself. An exterminator is the best person to deal with crawling insects, especially ants, roaches, and silverfish, provided they are not living in the plants' soil. Ants sometimes make their nests in large planters, destroying root systems and taking new growth from the plant. Roaches and silverfish usually live in floors and walls, far from your prying eyes, and though they really prefer to eat odd bits of leftover food, they are partial to the leaves of certain plants. Millipedes and centipedes, those horrible million-legged worm-like creatures, apart from making me jump 10 feet whenever I see one, are soil dwellers who love decayed vegetable matter and young roots. Soil drenches will wipe out these and other unwanted inhabitants of the soil, such as springtails (flea-like little bugs that hop around like miniature kangaroos), sowbugs (fat, grey little armadillos that run around the top of the pot when you water and that curl into balls when touched), and fungus gnats (either tiny larvae in the soil or grey-black flying adults that resemble fruit flies).

Whenever you suspect that an unwanted visitor is living in the soil, you should go into action:

1   Try to water your plants a little less; all soil bugs prefer damp, moist soil.

2   Use a recommended soil drench. These are mixed with the water you use for watering your plant. Three treatments, once every three weeks, are always more than any soil pest can handle.

51

Fungi, Moulds, and Mildew

These may be white, grey, green, orange, yellow—almost any colour—and may be smelled, if not seen. Some look like powder, others like miniature forests; all have been caused by too much moisture or stagnating water. Affected plants should be watered less, and not misted at all until the condition stops. (And you're lucky if the plant likes sunlight, for most moulds don't.) Fungicides are also very effective, especially for terrariums. Usually in powder form, fungicides can be dusted straight onto the infected spots on a house plant. For soil fungi, the fungicide should be mixed with water and the soil watered with the solution two or three times a few weeks apart; spray the same mixture into your terrarium every two weeks until the trouble clears up.

But let's hope you never get any of these nasties as house guests; if you do, the bugs you have just read about are the most common pests, and, unless life throws you a mean curve, you shouldn't meet up with any others. Now that I have told you how often to spray, I want you to learn how to use the pesticides properly.

Using Pesticides

Pesticides, when used properly, are a great help to the indoor gardener, but when used improperly, they spell certain death. Read the label. Never mind which type of pesticide you have chosen, *read the label* before you merrily spray away, killing your plant, your pet, and possibly yourself. Labels on all containers give warnings about what not to do; they also tell you which plants should not be sprayed with that particular type of pesticide. Follow these instructions to the letter.

All the pesticides I have mentioned in this chapter are in concentrated form and must be mixed with water before they can be used. I realize that there are a number of ready-mixed, pressurized, canned sprays on the market, and you may have wondered why I haven't recommended any of them. There are several reasons why not. First, they are ridiculously expensive—for only a little less than the cost of a whole box or bottle of concentrated pesticide, you get a few ounces of pressurized stuff that usually only lasts for one or two thorough sprayings, while the concentrates are capable of treating a large number of plants again and again. Second, I have yet to find a pressurized spray that was really effective. They do work, but I've found you have to spray a lot more often to get the same results. Third, so as not to damage the plant with the cold blast from these cans, you have to stay well away from what you are spraying, so that when you are trying to spray a plant with a lot of thick, interior growth, the job becomes almost impossible. And finally, some scientists are coming to the conclusion that cans with pressurized contents release undesirable gases that pollute the atmosphere. So don't let's use a pressurized spray if we don't have to!

'Mix 1 teaspoon to 1 quart of water.' When you read that statement, don't do anything but mix the pesticide *as directed*. A number of times clients of mine have thought that if one teaspoon was good, two teaspoons would be twice as good. They reason that they have a lot of bugs, so let's hit them hard with a doubly strong mixture the first time. Spooning twice as much pesticide as was called for into their container of water, they spray the infected plant vigorously. You can imagine their consternation the next day, when not only the bug, but the plant too, is quite dead.

The safest path to follow when spraying with a new pesticide is to test it directly on the plant before you finally make up your mind to use it. Mix some pesticide to the exact strength specified, take one branch of the infected plant, and spray it from top to bottom until it's dripping wet. Be careful not to get any spray on the rest of the plant; mark the sprayed branch with tape or string, then wait. If in three or four days the sprayed leaves do not show any sign of damage, then go ahead and use the pesticide on the remainder of the plant; but if the sprayed branch has begun to drop its leaves, or they are developing brown patches, it's time to go to the plant store for a substitute spray that might suit your plant better.

A pesticide can only be effective if it is properly used. The best pesticide in the world, if improperly applied, has little hope of doing its job. Because all bugs prefer the underside of the leaf or the shady areas of the branches and trunk away from the outside leaves of the plant, a quick spraying over the top of the leaves is totally useless. If this is what you intend to do, it would be better not to spray at all; save yourself all the fuss, smell, and bother of spraying, and leave the bugs to flourish. The correct way to spray any plant is to get your atomizer out, determine the volume of water it holds, mix in the pesticide according to instructions, and spray. Tip a small plant away from you, so that you can easily see the undersides of the leaves. Spray all the parts of the plant you can see, then give it a quarter turn, tip it again, and so on, all the way round. After you've done that, spray the tops of the leaves until you are sure no surface has been missed. Be certain to coat every stem and twig, and to aim the mist at every hole and crevice. As for large plants, obviously you are not going to hold the big fellow up in your hand. Instead, hold onto the pot and tip the plant away from you, again so that you can easily see the undersides of the leaves. If your atomizer has a nozzle adjustment, turn it until you get a spray that is long in reach but still fanned out, enabling you to reach the farthest tips. Spray every surface you can reach, then spray the top by walking around the plant or standing on a chair.

Spraying makes a terrible mess, and some pesticides contain oils that can stain fabrics, walls, and furniture. If it's summer, take the plant outdoors for its spraying. Do it on a patio or balcony, or in a driveway—anywhere that doesn't have plants nearby or from which you can remove other plants for a while. Remember, the pesticide you are using, although harmless to your infected plant, could wreak havoc with the lawn or your bedded flowers and shrubs. In cold weather, take the plant to a room where you can spray without too much worry: the basement, perhaps, or a large utility or recreation room. Spread out newspapers or a sheet of plastic before you start work.

All pesticide containers have the little skull and cross-bones symbol on the label; this means DANGER, POISON, and that's what it really does mean. Store the stuff out of the reach of children or pets. Always make sure the spraying area is well ventilated. Wear gloves when you're using a pesticide, because certain ingredients may enter your body through the skin. You may be allergic to other ingredients, or think you are; carried in the fumes, they can be highly irritating to sensitive breathing passages. Always aim the spray away from you, and not near pets' food or their resting spots. Wash carefully afterwards—wash off the counters and sink, too. Pesticides are perfectly safe when used properly; treat them with a healthy respect and you will never have any trouble.

Perhaps your little plant is a herb or vegetable destined for the table. If so, you really ought to use the organic method of pest control, I feel. Mist the plant heavily once a day, or bathe it in mild soapy water—again, real soap or soap flakes, not detergent—or immerse the whole top in soapy water and shake it vigorously, leaving it in for five

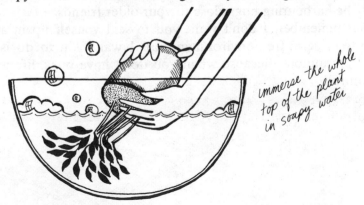

immerse the whole top of the plant in soapy water

minutes or so. If you do break down and use a pesticide, make sure it's specifically for vegetables and fruit, and never use systemics or soil drenches, because these enter the plant.

Preventive Measures

Aside from buying your own pests on your new house plants, there are other ways they can get their little feet in at your door. Throughout the year you can buy fabulous potted and cut flowers to brighten up your home. I'm all in favour of this—I buy them, too. Whenever you buy flowers, especially potted ones, be careful not to put them near any of your good old standbys. Mums with aphids and red spiders are not uncommon, and you wouldn't believe what I've seen lurking under pretty primulas and hanging onto hyacinths—in fact, I've seen creatures in or on nearly every kind of flower for sale. But take courage: pests on potted flowers are not a disastrous tragedy. Usually the flowers only last a week, possibly two weeks, and when the flowers go, the plant goes, too. So stand that pot of mums 5 to 10 feet away from your other plants, then the chances of infection will be slim.

Keep house plants away from physical contact with nearby outside plants in window boxes or balcony gardens, or other plants that are just next to the window. Again, use common sense, and don't bring any stranger that could possibly be harbouring bugs close to your older friends.

But remember, I don't want you to seal youself up in a bug-free, germ-free environment—all I want you to do is take precautions, because when you don't have bugs, life is beautiful!

6

After the Battle

Poor old Alfred! Think back to seven months ago, when he arrived: shiny, crisp leaves proudly sticking out in all directions. Didn't he look great next to the sofa—so stately, so serene, that you named him Alfred because he reminded you of a butler. Alfred lost a few leaves until you learned to water him right, but he was great! Then came his illness— and did those creeps ever do a lot of damage before you even noticed the trouble. When you finally got rid of the bugs, Alfred looked stark naked: just a clump of green at the top and a skinny stick down into the soil. Your once-beautiful companion now looks tired, old, and skinny. Poor Alfred. And now what can you do? Shrug your shoulders and chuck him out? Never! Save him! Regrowing a plant can be considered an act of devotion.

When you buy a plant, it either looks this way or that way, but with an Alfred, you have the choice. You want him short, round, and bushy, or maybe tall and slim, or perhaps gracefully leaning to one side like the ones on your Willow Pattern teacups? Go ahead, create; the decision is yours. All it takes is time, for plants grow slowly. Patience is an important element, and when you add some perseverance˙ to it, you can't fail. Good; now that I have charged you with enthusiasm, let's go.

Pruning, Pinching, Air Layering

The first few swipes of your scissors or pruning shears will alter a plant's shape for years to come. Obviously, the way to begin is to snip off all the dead branches, twigs, stems, and leaves. But just because a stem has no leaves on it, don't assume that it's dead; it may only be resting from an ordeal and waiting to regain the inspiration and the strength to burst out again with lots of green! When you're not sure, cut back 2 or 3 inches at the end and inspect them for 'bleeding' (by that I mean the running of the plant juices), which indicates life. Not all plants 'bleed', so look for a green ring just under the bark, or any greenness at all. Anything that is brown and dry, brittle, grey and withered, or black, is probably dead. So always start at the tip of the branch, cutting back one short length at a time until you reach the living matter.

When you can see a moist, greenish look to the stem, you have removed all the useless and expendable material, so stop cutting. If your plant is completely denuded (entirely leafless), put it aside for a few months; give it free rein to fill out a bit before you attempt any more major reshaping. But if it still looks pretty thick, so you have a lot to work with, don't be afraid to don your artist's beret and hew the plant into the shape you like. You might want to trim off all the branches that stick out beyond the fat, round, basketball

shape you have pictured in your mind's eye, or prefer to snip off all the lower elderly branches, leaving a fresh green umbrella shape at the top. Pruning has the same effect as pinching: a branch that has been pruned is forced to branch out even more, filling in the empty spaces. For small plants, and for vines and creepers, pruning is absolutely necessary. If a small, non-climbing plant has lost its leaves, the best course is to cut it back to its major 'Y' joint. The long trailing end-growths of vines and creepers should be trimmed back to the point where the plants look substantial again, or to just a few inches beyond the edge of the pot.

After pruning, a plant will try to grow outwards and up from the ends of its branches, leaving its centre bare and unsightly, so that pinching is definitely needed.

Air layering is a safe way to get green leaves from up top and bring them down below. I went to see a client who has owned a *Dracaena massangeana* for nineteen years. He bought it when his wife gave birth to their second son. The second son is now 6 feet tall, and going to university. The Dracaena is 8 feet tall, and prefers not to leave the soft life it has at home. The sole problem for my client's tallest family member is the ceiling; its height is only 7 feet 9 inches, and the Dracaena is therefore a bit cramped. But, through the miracle of air layering, my client now has a plant 4 feet 6 inches high, with three growing points instead of just one.

To perform the operation called air layering, you need:

1. a quantity of moss called sphagnum moss (not as rare as it sounds; it's obtainable at most nurseries or plant stores)

2. a small wedge-shaped stick with a pointed end, about 4 or 5 inches long

3. some plastic

4. some string

5. a sharp knife with a strong blade

6. a pair of scissors

The best place to air layer on your ultra-tall (say 7- or 8-foot, anyway) gangly long-stemmed plant is from 3 to 4 feet down from the top; a cut here will still leave you with a tall plant and a large enough piece for another. What you are trying to do is to get the top half to grow roots; when it has grown roots, you cut the top off *under* the new roots and plant it.

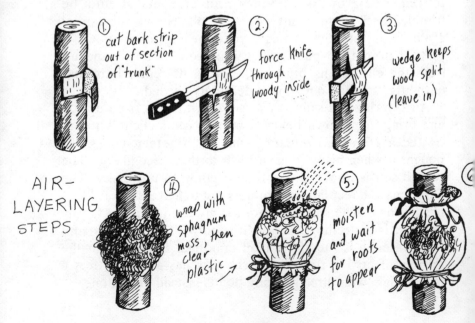

1. cut bark strip out of section of "trunk"

2. force knife through woody inside

3. wedge keeps wood split (leave in)

AIR-LAYERING STEPS

4. wrap with sphagnum moss, then clear plastic

5. moisten and wait for roots to appear

6.

With your sharp knife, cut a piece out of the bark layer of the plant: a section that's about 2 inches deep and that goes about three-quarters of the way around the stem. Leave a strip of bark still connecting the top of the plant with the bottom of the plant. Never cut a full ring around the stem: this is called 'skirting', and it spells certain death for the top half of the plant because all the flow of life-giving sap is in the bark, and if you interrupt the flow completely, the top will die.

That was the first step—now for the second. Hold your knife blade parallel to the piece of remaining bark, and slowly force the knife through the centre wood until it comes out the other side. Then force your wedge-shaped stick into the cut until you can see it appearing through the other side. Leave the stick there. Take a good handful of sphagnum moss and wrap it all around the wound, making sure that the moss extends 2 or 3 inches both above and below the missing bark. Wrap the moss with clear plastic and tie it snugly at the bottom with string. Water the moss liberally and pull the plastic tight at the top, securing it either by wrapping it in on itself or by holding it with a garbage-bag tie. You should be able to reopen the top easily, because the moss ought to be checked at least once a week to make sure it's still moist. If you are careful not to let the moss dry out, 6 to 9 weeks later you will notice roots growing into it, or showing through the plastic. Besides shortening a tall plant, air layering is invaluable for filling out the bottom of a plant that has lost all its lower leaves. The stalk that has had its top lopped off will send out a new growing point—possibly even two or more new ones—to replace it.

Cuttings

Pruning your plant usually leaves you with a number of healthy cuttings. If you have taken these from a plant that is now anything but a picture of health, the cuttings may be

dark-tinted
bottle

cloth-wrapped
jar →

← pot of moist sand
covered with clear plastic

the only way the original plant can extend its existence. Cuttings can be successfully rooted in any of three mediums: water, moist sand, or soil. The first two are excellent for nearly all vines, creepers, and softwood plants. (A softwood plant has no wood within the main stem—it's usually green in colour right through. Coleus and Dieffenbachia are softwood plants.) Soil should be used for hardwoods, such as *Ficus benjamina*. To ensure success, a rooting hormone, available at most garden stores, is helpful. Perhaps you are undecided which is the best method; if you are, you might split the cuttings up into three groups, and try out all three mediums as experiments.

For the water method, use dechlorinated water and select a dark-tinted bottle (one that has contained vitamins, perhaps, or a beer bottle) or wrap a clear-glass bottle in a cloth to keep light, especially hot sunlight, away from the infant roots. Look at the water—and smell it, too—once a week. If it looks clear and smells fresh, you need not worry, but if it is discoloured, has a film on top, or unpleasant deposits seem to be forming at the edges, or if it smells like pond slime, then hurry to wash out the container and replace it with fresh, dechlorinated water. Be sure to pull off any leaves that are in or under the water. A leaf totally immersed in water soon rots, making it all the more easy for your water to go bad.

Being a thrifty soul, I have always found that I get more cuttings for my cutting dollar if I cut, say, three 12-inch pieces into six 6-inch pieces. Apart from increasing the number of potential plants, the larger number of pieces increases the ratio of success, since a few out of any batch of cuttings just don't 'take' for one reason or another. So if you have twenty-five 12-inch pieces, there could be plenty of 6-inch pieces for your friends, as well.

Repotting

A dedicated indoor gardener repots his little ones once a year, his large ones once every two years—and all of them as early in spring as possible. Before I discuss soil and how to approach it, let's chat about that important activity called repotting. I have seen many a white knuckle, chewed fingernail, and pale face, all because I suggested a client repot this or that plant. Repotting is not difficult; repotting is *easy*—easier than trying to figure out how to water your plants correctly, for example. All well-behaved plants hold the soil in the pot in place with their roots, forming what is called a 'root ball'. When turned out of the pot, the soil and roots have a solid, compact shape—they may even come out without even one little bit of earth falling off. It's so easy; come on, try it!

Choosing the right pot is the first concern. Don't ever assume that if it's a big pot it's a good pot. How sad a 3-inch-high seedling looks in an 18-inch pot: a small green speck in the centre of a sea of soil. Poor lonely little thing. The proud owner of this young hopeful has probably reasoned to himself or herself that because the seedling is going to be a tree, it had better be put into a big enough pot. I

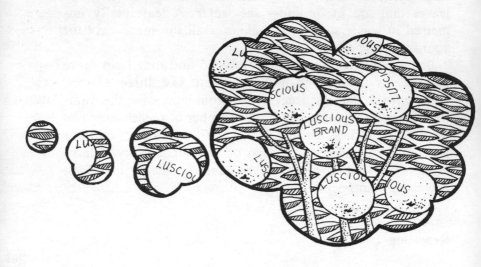

think these people must be hoping for a visitation from the Large Tree Fairy, who will wave her magic wand in the moonlight—and that little grapefruit pip, with its two leaves, will instantly grow 7 feet tall, a thousand more leaves, and fifty ripe, luscious grapefruits! Plants like to feel their limitations; in fact, some plants insist on being a little pot-bound or they won't grow any foilage to speak of. Measure the old pot, then choose one that's 2 inches deeper, and 2 inches wider in diameter (which works out to an inch larger all round, if you think about it)—an increase that doesn't sound very much; but if you're using a very large pot you may use 10 pounds of soil trying to fill in that extra 2 inches, and 10 pounds will give the plant quite enough extra growing space.

There are pots with drainage holes and pots without. They come in different materials: plastic, clay, metal, glazed china, fiberglas, and many others. Pots with drainage are best for your plants because excess water can run out of the bottom. Pots without drainage (they're sometimes called solid-bottom planters) are a little more tricky to use, but if you know how, they are good, too. When you are preparing a pot with a drainage hole, make sure the hole does not accidentally become blocked with soil; to prevent this, put a few shards (pieces of broken pots) or some fairly large stones over the hole. Cover these with an inch or so of soil, then carefully put in the complete root ball and fill in the space between it and the sides of the pot with soil. The crown, or neck, of the plant (that's the part between the root and the stem—it's usually at ground level) should be slightly lower than the rim; never cover it up with more soil. If there are a number of drainage holes at the sides of the pot, fill the bottom of the pot with shards or stones to a point just above them. But a layer of stones in any large container will make the whole thing weigh a ton, and if you plan to be fairly regular about your repotting, large chips of bark mulch work very well instead. Bark mulch chips are chunks of cedar or fir bark, and are available in large sacks from garden supply houses. If you tend to be forgetful about repotting, better stick to the stones, though, because the bark

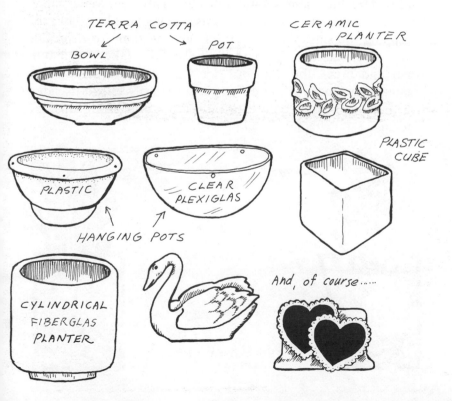

TERRA COTTA

BOWL   POT

CERAMIC PLANTER

PLASTIC

CLEAR PLEXIGLAS

PLASTIC CUBE

HANGING POTS

CYLINDRICAL FIBERGLAS PLANTER

And, of course......

will eventually rot and no longer provide the very necessary drainage. When you are moving your plant from a pot with drainage to one without, the new solid-bottom planter should be at least 4 inches deeper than the pot that had drainage. The extra inches in depth are needed for reservoir purposes—if you are a chronic over-waterer, the root ball itself will remain somewhat dry, as it should. Put in at least 2 inches of drainage materials (shards or stones), along with a few pieces of charcoal for freshness. Pack this material down tightly, so that the soil will not seep through the crevices. A layer of perlite or vermiculite over the stones might be your best bet in helping to keep the soil where it belongs.

To remove your plant from its outgrown terra cotta pot, spread out one hand over the entire top of the pot to hold the contents in, and, with your free hand, pick up the pot and turn it and its contents upside-down. Then rap the rim of the pot smartly on the edge of the counter, water tap, or table, and the plant should fall out easily into your hand. For the stubborn plant that resists leaving its old home, try slapping the sides and bottom of the pot, then hit it on the edge of the table again. And if all else fails, take your hammer and break the pot—but don't hit it so hard that you damage the roots. If the pot is plastic, simply knead its sides in and out a little before turning the whole thing upside-down.

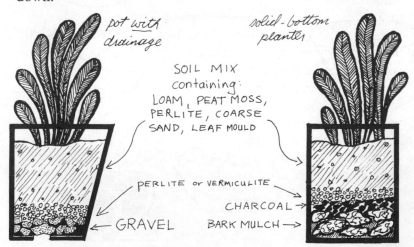

pot with drainage

solid-bottom planter

SOIL MIX containing: LOAM, PEAT MOSS, PERLITE, COARSE SAND, LEAF MOULD

PERLITE or VERMICULITE

← GRAVEL

CHARCOAL →

BARK MULCH →

When I think about soils, I am at once reminded of my first large Areca Palm, which I named Annebelle. I believe my mother intended me to convert her birthday money into socks and underwear, so it seemed appropriate to name my new plant after her. Annebelle was perfection for about eight months—until the spring, when I decided it was time to repot my beauty. Instead of buying sterilized soil, I purchased the best dark loam I had ever seen, from a huge pile sitting beside an Italian vegetable store. I mixed my loam with sand, peat moss, and other goodies, and carefully repotted Annebelle. Unfortunately for her, I was still learning how to grow house plants, and in the early stages I was a pupil in the School of Hard Knocks. That superb black loam would have been ideal to spread over a lawn, or dig into flower beds, but to use it on a house plant was a disaster of Titanic proportions. After one month in her new soil, Annebelle was enduring chewed roots from hungry sowbugs and millipedes, and a fantastic case of scale and mealybug. When the clouds of dust finally rose from the battlefield that was Annebelle, she had been reduced to half her former beautiful self. And I can already hear you saying to yourself, in a voice of horror, 'I don't want to have anything like that happen to *my* prize—what is sterilized soil?'

Sterilized soil is soil that has been baked or steamed for a number of hours at between 180 and 200°F (that's about 82 to 93°C), to ensure that all beasties, bacteria, and their potential offspring have been annihilated. Soil sterilizers can be purchased, or you can even use your oven, but I suggest you don't try any home sterilization unless you have a detached work area in which to do it. Soil that is being baked sometimes gives off unbelievably foul odours. Anyway, prepackaged sterilized soil is relatively cheap, and unless you are potting hundreds of plants, it is not economical to buy a soil sterilizer. Before I continue, here's one more statement, this time on soil from outdoors, directed at people who dwell on ground that contains a large quantity of clay. Even if your back yard has a lot of clay in the soil, you can dig it up each year, mix it with topsoil, and watch your garden grow. That's *outside*. *Inside* is quite a different matter. Clay soil in a pot turns to stone indoors: water either sits on the top, barely sinking in, or the soil shrinks away from the sides of the pot. The water rushes down through the gap around the soil and either out through the bottom of the pot or into the drainage reservoir (if the pot is a solid-bottom planter), leaving the root ball virtually untouched. Your plant may survive, but it won't thrive.

A hopeful plant novice, when confronted by the unbelievably wide selection of additives that can be mixed with the soil, is immediately confused. Row upon row of bags and boxes of mosses, starting mediums, leaf moulds, manures, sand, and many more. These racks of ingredients seem to call for such precision—making you suspect that if you don't mix exactly right, you will be dogged only by failure. Don't worry, it's not that bad—besides, for most repotting, the work has been done for you. There are many general-purpose potting soils on the market that are sterilized and that have been mixed with everything your plant's little roots could desire. Read the label: if the soil has been sterilized and contains some perlite, peat moss, and sand, excellent—buy it; but steer clear of anything that could double as kitty litter. Unless I have a plant that needs a rare, special type of soil, I usually use premixed soil myself. I trust it, it works well, and besides, I sometimes need a bit of extra time for some other chore—or just feel plain lazy!

Now to explain why soil should contain sand, moss, and perlite, as well as good old earth. Peat moss is coarse, light, and springy; it helps prevent the soil from compacting. It's absorbent, and, best of all, its chemical properties promote root growth. Peat moss also provides spaces for air and oxygen, and substance in which the roots can get a firm footing. Sand (builders' coarse-grained sand, not fine beach sand, which packs too easily) provides fast drainage, thus preventing pockets of water from collecting in the soil. Its heavy, gritty texture makes a solid anchor and ballast—your Aspidistra won't keel over. Perlite is light, and does all that sand does, as well as absorbing water; it then releases the water when the soil begins to dry. A soil mix containing all these is right for most plants.

If you do decide to whip up your own special blend, use sterilized soil, peat moss, and coarse sand in equal parts. When you have mixed enough for the job, throw in about a handful of perlite and mix it in too until the soil is flecked lightly with white spots. As an added treat, like being given ice cream—with a wedge of pie, substitute a handful or so of leaf mould for a handful or two of soil while mixing. Leaf mould consists of decayed leaves and organic material—plants love it. But use it in moderation, as you do pie!

For cacti and plants that require a fast-drying soil, use two parts sand to one of soil, and just enough peat moss so they don't feel deprived of nutrition: say one handful to six of the rest. Add some perlite, as I've just mentioned. Plants that like moist soil prefer two parts soil to two parts peat moss to one of sand, and, of course, our good old friend, perlite. Simple.

The pH factor, in other words the acid and alkaline content of the soil, is something a novice should not worry about. To begin with, it's difficult to know just where your soil stands on the scale, and to find out, you must test it with a complicated kit or meter. Then you have to discover the

pH needs of your plant, and after that adjust the soil up or down the scale accordingly. All one big fussy nuisance, and frankly you shouldn't even have to think about this aspect of potting. If you do come across a plant that clamours for higher acidity—for instance, a lemon tree that's losing the chlorophyll (green colour) in its leaves—you can adjust your soil to acid by adding more peat moss to the mix. If you have a plant that sulks because it needs a more alkaline soil, add lime, very sparingly; some alkaline-loving plants can be encouraged to bloom with a little lime.

Fertilizing

Bags and boxes of fertilizers are labelled with three numbers which give, in percentages, the proportions of the three major ingredients: nitrogen, phosphorus, and potassium(potash). In very simple terms, nitrogen makes leaves green and encourages them to grow; phosphorus provides for stem and root development, and potassium for stem and flower development. Of course these three elements do much more than that, but let's keep it simple. As well as the three essentials, a good fertilizer should contain trace elements—very small amounts of minerals or substances that plants need to help them grow, and (especially) to prevent deficiencies. An otherwise healthy plant, when deficient in a needed trace element, won't develop in the way it should.

Fertilizers are essential for growth, but when mixed too strong and used too often they cause trouble. Please refrain from being over-enthusiastic in using them. Follow the instructions on the label—never use fertilizers at a greater strength or more often than is recommended; in fact, you should tend to use them less often. I recommend you fertilize no more than once a month, even if the instructions indicate that more frequent use might be a good thing. Don't fertilize during the winter months (November to mid-March) when plants are resting a bit, or at least prefer not being forced to 'eat and grow big and tall'. Don't regularly fertilize a plant that's not showing steady growth – the unused buildup of sediment from the fertilizer may eventually burn the roots. Instead, fertilize once, then wait until the plant has begun to grow again before you give it any more. Fertilizers should be mixed with your regular plant water, then administered as one portion in your weekly watering schedule. For instance, the instructions may say 'Use 1 teaspoon per gallon'. If you usually water your plants three times a week, giving them about 2 pints between them each time, just add a quarter of a teaspoon of the fertilizer to their usual water once a week. 'Use 1 teaspoon per gallon' doesn't mean you have to pour a whole gallon over them.

My favourite way of fertilizing is to use a combination of chemical and organic fertilizers. Most indoor leafy plants respond favourably to a balanced fertilizer such as 20-20-20, and I haven't met a plant yet that didn't enjoy a little fish fertilizer every now and again. Fish fertilizer is just that: decomposed fish matter in liquid form. You don't buy it at a Tropical Fish Emporium as many people assume, but at an ordinary plant store. Fish fertilizer is good value because it contains a host of trace elements, vitamins, and minerals, as well as other natural or organic extras which make your plants grow with joy. And it's a fern's best friend: any fern really loves the stuff. I suggest you give ferns (but no other type of plant) fertilizer more often than once a month. When your fern is growing, give it fish fertilizer *twice* a month. As for all your other plants, fertilize once a month with 20-20-20 and fish fertilizer, alternating from one to the other each month.

Finally we come to your flowering plants, which need to be fertilized too. African violets, geraniums, begonias, to name the most common, should be given a fertilizer formulated to encourage development of blooms either just before they are supposed to bloom or when you see the first bud. A number of fertilizers state that they are specifically for this purpose, and you can easily check this by looking at the series of three numbers printed on the package: the first one in the series should be low, while the numbers representing phosphorus and potassium should be high.

Winter and Summer

Canada doesn't fool around with her seasons, especially in the inland provinces. From the hum of the air conditioners in the oppressive heat of summer to the growl of the furnaces to offset our frigid winters, we and our plants are really expected to run the full gamut of weather conditions. The statement that winter time is dormancy time appears in many plant books, especially those written in Europe. When winter comes to the Europeans, most of their homes become cooler, growth of their plants begins to slow down and, in especially cool conditions, some plants may stop growing altogether. The temperature of the average room may be perhaps 48 to 68°F (about 9 to 20°C)—temperatures that tend to provoke dormancy—and the plants behave like good children and go to sleep. In Canada, our plants are still bright-eyed and bushy-tailed in the middle of January—not because we Canadians raise rebellious and spoiled plants that won't do as they're told, but because our furnaces really go to work. In my apartment it's hotter in winter than it is in summer. Great hissing, clanging radiators, which look like fugitives from a Jules Verne novel, belch out heat night and day. No plant in its right mind is going to go dormant in that kind of heat. This extreme winter heat truly is unfortunate, for although the warmth may be there, nothing else is: the air is crackling dry, the sun is hopelessly weak. But if perhaps you keep your house cooler than average, and your plants do stop growing in the winter, wonderful—throw a party, call your family, do home improvements in your spare time: you are one of the lucky ones.

Dormancy is good for your plant in the same way that a good night's sleep is good for you. A plant that has been allowed two or three months of dormancy has had a chance to store his energies in reserve for the new growing season. When spring arrives, he almost bursts out of his pot with new growth, like a jack-in-the-box. If you are able to place your plant in a cool room, say 45 to 60°F (7 to 16°C), and in moderate to low light, he will go dormant. A dormant plant generally loses a few leaves, and looks dishevelled and unkempt while inactive. Water your dormant plants much less than your growing plants (either smaller amounts or less often) and don't fertilize them, but *do* feel optimistic. After about three months, bring them out, repot them, put them in their usual spots, and watch them grow.

For those of us who don't have a cool place for our plants, a hot indoor winter is a time of worry, work, and possible disappointment. Our main concern is to fight the dry air. The constant swishing sound of humidifiers and vaporizers can be heard in my apartment throughout the winter. Besides using humidifiers, mist your plants once a day at least, twice if you have the time and patience. There is so little daylight in the winter; gloomy skies seem to last forever. If your plants are still growing, move them closer to the window to prevent that scraggly, wan, winter appearance. Don't fertilize even the growing plant in winter—we *want* him to slow down. And contrary to the laws of dormancy and nature, you will probably have to water these plants a little more in winter because dry air soaks up soil moisture so much faster than does damp air.

Though we all have a hard time of it in winter, we can really benefit from the summer. Strong light and humid air make our plants flourish and grow vigorously. If you take your plants outside in the summer and leave them out for a few months, any sickly plant will happily regain its former beauty. Being outdoors is a ready-made cure for shabby winter looks or the after-effects of bugs. Your plant will enjoy the cool, dark nights and the dew and rain, but you must be careful of the sun itself—setting him down on an unshaded concrete patio is not cricket. On a particularly hot day, you can effectively roast your friend's leaves, branches, and roots. Unless you are quite certain the plant you own enjoys full, direct sun, don't put him in a place that receives noonday sun. The best spots are those that receive either early morning sun (until ten o'clock, say) or late afternoon sun (not before three o'clock at the earliest). During the rest of the day, your plant should be sheltered by a tree, wall, fence, solid partition, or closed-in balcony railing—anything. Pots should be checked to see if they are drying out like hotcakes at least once every second day. If you can, try to stand your plant on either grass or soil, because asphalt, concrete, and wood decks get much too hot. It's painful enough for you to walk barefoot on these materials in summer, so imagine what your plant thinks of it—even when wearing an earthenware pot. None of us likes hot feet.

Plants can go outdoors between May and September; then, in late September, you have to try to get them indoors again with the least amount of shock to their systems. About a week before bringing them in, it is a good idea to move them to a place where there is very little direct sunlight or none at all. After that, take them indoors to a bright spot, wait another week, and move them to their original standing places.

House plants really enjoy their vacations, and these, if planned properly, will reward you with more luxuriant healthier plants. And (need I say it) don't forget to check for tiny, plant-eating passengers; wash off the plants with a garden hose before bringing them back inside.

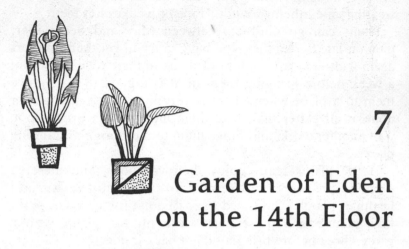

7

Garden of Eden
on the 14th Floor

Plant design—my hobby as well as part of my work, and a part that I especially enjoy. Nothing is more fun than creating an arrangement of plants, by hanging a few, moving others, using artificial light, suggesting that a few new ones be added, or even that one or two be quietly removed.

Plants, properly and imaginatively used, can add great warmth to an otherwise cold contemporary interior, can give additional elegance to a traditional room, or liven up a bleak office; but improperly used they can make a room look scruffy, unkempt, or poorly planned. And there is such a thing as having too many plants—though I know you may find this statement hard to believe, coming from me. I have met enthusiasts who love plants so much that their homes seem to have become replicas of an impenetrable jungle. You crouch and dodge through the room, crawl under the palm to sit on the sofa; you talk through a wall of green to the person you are reasonably certain is sitting over there—somewhere; you hit your head on the bottoms of hanging plants; you can't even find the bathroom. In fact, after being in a place like this for a while, you begin to wish you had brought along a compass and survival kit. You really can have too many plants.

Then there is the improper use of plants. I've seen what appears to be a 3-inch snippet of green standing all alone in a room the size of an aircraft hangar, and a huge, spreading, 10-foot plant squeezed into a room the size of a shoebox. Plants should enhance their surroundings; they should add life and colour to a room without disturbing the overall look or impeding the efficient use of work areas. Choose your plants, thinking where you want to put them, and set them in their places with the same care you take in arranging furniture.

In the world of commercial interior design, there are designers who do nothing more than arrange the contents of a room to provide maximum efficiency and ease of use. These designers are called 'space planners'. They make sure you can open that drawer without knocking your knee, overturning the wastebasket, or doing anything that might cause inconvenience to an otherwise well-run office. When you are placing new plants in your home, especially hanging plants, a little space planning can save a lot of grief. In a cartoon, it can be funny when someone gets hit on the head with a flowerpot; in real life it's unfortunate and possibly dangerous. So when hanging that pot, think of the amount and type of traffic the area usually gets. If it's the runway for your kids (between that favourite chair and the rest of the room), or any other area in constant use (perhaps over the washing machine), don't hang it there.

One more 'don't', then I'll start on the 'do's'. I have a friend who is a nut for the symmetrical placement of objects. In *her* cupboards, plates are exactly 3 inches apart from each other; objects of varying heights, such as books, flow along her bookshelves from the tallest to the shortest, without even a rise or a bump. When plants are placed symmetrically, the look is certainly organized, but rather regimented; after all, some plants are spiky, some are fluffy, and grouping the pots in strict order cancels out the natural, spontaneous quality of an arrangement.

Small plants may be grouped close together in one spot to

think of the type
of traffic the area
usually gets.....

create a burst of green. Four or five of them at one side of a
shelf, foliage arranged so that their pots are all but covered
in leaves, will create a tropical garden all their own. Of
course, if you put the tallish ones at the back and the trailing
ones in front, they will all be shown to best advantage, but
you need never place them *exactly* according to height. Little plants look delightful in interesting containers—in low
bowls, or in baskets, china animals with hollow centres, or
any other eye-catching knickknack. I love to make hanging
arrangements of very small plants in very small pots: a
couple of tiny plants, hung at different heights just to one
side of a big one, give a sun, moon, and stars effect. I've also
seen fascinating miniature gardens, consisting of a bunch of
incredibly small thimble-sized pots containing incredibly
small plants, grouped in a saucer or some other low, flat
container and standing on a coffee table. These Lilliputian
displays are very charming and touching. A solitary small
plant should be placed in a cosy little nook or cranny, where
he looks a bit too big for his home. Nothing looks more
forlorn than a 2-inch-high green thing all alone on a 12-
foot-long windowsill. One last trick with small plants: you
can make big plants out of them. Five or six little 59¢ plants,
of the same or similar types, planted in an 8-inch pot, suddenly transform themselves into a medium-sized plant. And
don't forget that a whole area can be filled with several

... this is
a bathroom

medium-sized plants for much less than the cost of just one big one.

You'll be familiar with the placid feeling that comes over you when you sit on the grass among the wildflowers under the spreading branches of a tree, and look out at all the beauty and splendour that is nature. Well, the proper use of plants indoors can also bring you this feeling of restfulness and inner peace. If at all possible, try to place your best (and best-loved) display of greenery where you and your friends are certain to see it when you are using the room. Also, when possible, arrange the plants so that they can be seen not only when you enter the room but also while you are conversing or dining. It's whatever we see *first* that creates the immediate impression—of well-being, for us, since we're discussing green plants. For instance, a luxuriant display of plants directly in the line of vision from an entrance can create the impression of a greenhouse, even if these are the only plants in the room. An appropriately placed cluster of four or five plants can create more of a tropical feel than twenty or more poorly displayed ones.

When you marvel at natural wonders—Lake Louise in Banff National Park, the shore of Lake Superior, or the eastern seaboard, perhaps—it is because nature has given you such spectacular colours and formations to look at, and so many of them. Some of her wonders may be close to you, some far away, others high in the air or near the ground. Just so much to see, the small as well as the great, you have to get excited! But how can we create the same kind of emotion by using a few plants at home as nature creates by offering such abundant beauty in the wild? It can be done, though of course on a much smaller scale. One way is to make a very attractive multi-level planting. Just standing your plants on the floor will not always show them off to best advantage; suppose they are all mostly the same height, or all low to the ground, and you can't produce the effect you want—what then? Your answer: terracing—in other words, multi-level planting. There are any number of chrome, brass, aluminum, or plastic cylinders you can buy, all good looking, to set your plants at different heights, but all of them have one thing in common: they are extremely expensive. If you don't mind spending a lot, well and good, use these planters; but for the more thrifty minded there are several other ways of creating a terraced planting.

One really cheap and handsome way of terracing is to use baskets. Most basket shops have, of course, a wide variety of widths, heights, and types to choose from. Buy several baskets of varying sizes, and you are all set! You will probably have to put a stand of some sort into the tall baskets to hold up the pot and its saucer. A roll of corrugated cardboard, fitted low enough into the basket that the whole pot is below the rim of wicker, works well for everything but a very

TORTOISE - SHELL WEAVE   CANE WASTE-BASKET   RUSH BASKET   LAUNDRY HAMPER

heavy plant. Old bricks will do, if you don't plan to move often. Then cover the tops of the pots with bark mulch, and there you are! By the way, when using wicker, you must either put in catch trays or line the inside of the basket with plastic, otherwise the water run-off may rot the basket or the floor, and will certainly make a mess. A tray or some plastic is a good idea even if the plant already sits on a saucer.

A second method of terracing, which looks professional and is inexpensive, is to use terra cotta or cement flue drains. These are easily obtainable from your local lumber yard or builders' supply store. They come in square or round lengths of from 12 to 36 inches and in diameters (widths) of from 6 to 24 inches. A large one completely conceals an ugly utility metal pot in great style. A number of flue drains of varying heights creates a striking indoor garden. The terra cotta has a natural appearance but is very clean looking, blending well with either a modern interior or one furnished mainly with antiques. Cement flue drains are elegant in their own right as a modern medium but, like the terra cotta drains, can also be painted.

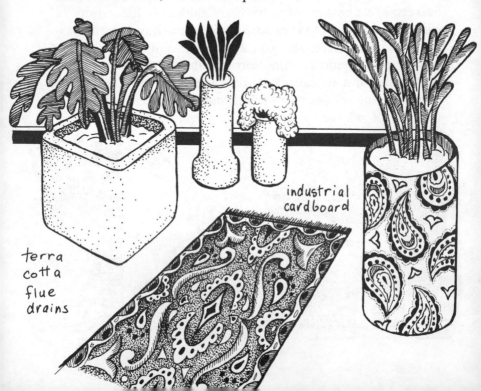

industrial cardboard

terra cotta flue drains

Another medium for terracing is the cardboard sleeve used to pour concrete pillars for buildings. The sleeve is a cylinder of heavy plastic-coated cardboard, usually sold in 12-foot lengths and in widths of 8 and 14 inches. One of these should do the job for you. The sleeve is easily cut with a saw, although once you have done this you are still far from finished: the cardboard must be covered with paper or cloth to disguise the printed surface and the spiral groove running around the outside. A thick wallpaper or fabric makes an attractive finish.

When you are setting up an indoor garden, it's not entirely necessary to buy new plants. Sometimes, with a little forethought, you can obtain the desired effect with what you have at hand. One client of mine had a really good idea, which I'll share with you. Years ago, when she was a little girl, she took her 25¢ allowance to a church bazaar, but try as she might, the only treasure she could buy with her money was a small rose-shaped Sansevieria. Through the years it reproduced, then its young grew more young, until finally, when she left home, she had boxes of them! She said that at first she tried to line them up on windowsills. In her words, 'That was a joke.' Then, like a bolt from the blue, the big idea struck. She built a ramp with steps coming down from her window, and filled each step with Sansevierias. The result was a fantastic sloping hill of green-and-white rosettes.

Sansevierias

Everyone has gone crazy about hanging plants: I think some people would cover their whole ceiling with them, if they could. Hang your plants at different levels and at different distances from the window. As well as the trailing plants, use some upright ones—they look at home in hanging pots, too. Try not to have too much difference in the colours of the pots and styles of hangers when you are arranging a group: five different shades of pots hung on five types of hangers makes the whole effect look a bit too 'busy'. But if you like making and mixing different types of pots and hangers, how about trying a whole display of the *same* plants in your different pots?

Artificial Lighting

On my bookshelves I have a whole slew of books: some fat, some skinny, some almost too technical, but all dealing with the complicated art of how best to light house plants artificially. Artificial light is a foolproof way to get plants to grow in dark, dingy hallways, but since we are talking about good plant design, let's not make the same mistake as some enthusiastic indoor gardeners, when they ruin an otherwise comfortable room with searing, blinding, unnatural-looking light.

The fluorescent lamp is the type of light considered most satisfactory by indoor lighting experts. Four years ago I constructed a wall unit in my living room, consisting of two double-tube 36-inch-long neon fixtures, a valance to cover the brutes, and a long metal tray in which I put stones and water, placed 12 inches below the lamps. This unit, equipped with a timer, I use as a combination seedling and cutting grower, as well as a 'yes, I'm home' device to confuse any would-be crooks. My seedlings grow bigger every day, enjoying 600 to 800 foot-candles of light for a sixteen-hour period. My unit is just what is needed for the plants, but a horrible pain to my friends and me, because directly across

*... under
the lights*

from it, and lower, is the couch we all most enjoy sitting on.
I think man is related to moths, somehow, because in the
same way that moths are attracted to light bulbs, human
eyes are attracted to fluorescent tubes. Like zombies we sit,
talking about our latest adventures, our eyes constantly fixed
on the glow from my wall unit. I'm forced to turn it off
when I'm entertaining, which isn't particularly good for my
plants. Unless you can place your light fixtures where they
cannot be seen directly from any of the usual sitting places,
don't use them. Another disadvantage of fluorescent lights is
that they have to be very close to the plants you are lighting
—a plant more than 12 inches away is not really getting
enough light. An advantage, though, is that the leaves don't
burn when they come in contact with these cooler lights.
Whether you're using fluorescent lights for seedlings or to
provide a 'plant hospital' for your sick plants, it is best to set
them up in a little-used room or basement. Hang them on
adjustable chains, keep them 3 to 6 inches away from the
tops of the plants, have the unit turned on for twelve to
sixteen hours a day (not twenty-four hours: plants like to
sleep, too), and all your greenery will grow beautifully for
you.

The best indoor lights for a well-designed room arrangement are spotlights, but the one hazard to watch out for with
these is heat. The best strength for spotlights is 150 to 175
watts, but even a 100-watt spotlight that's 12 inches away

from the plants it's lighting will successfully roast the tops off nine out of ten plants. Spotlights should be no closer to a plant than 3 feet, and no further than 5 feet away from it. If you want to use just one spotlight with a built-in reflector, that's all right; they are good, and inexpensive. I've found that specially manufactured bulbs said to be ideal for encouraging plants to grow may sell for twice the price of the usual old spotlight bulbs—but don't seem to do any more or less good. To my mind they are an added or unjustified expense.

Track lighting may be used very effectively for lighting your indoor plants. The best ones have reflectors or dish-reflectors; another type, directional-type spotlights, are probably best of all because they concentrate a lot of light in a small area. Whenever you are lighting plants artificially, watch for signs of poor growth (probably caused by insufficient light) and burned leaf-tops on your more sensitive plants. The best way to look after an artificially lit plant is to

let it change places every three or four months with a plant receiving natural light.

A few tips for anyone who may own an office or be in some kind of business premises: plants are great, here, and a well-landscaped office interior is a wonder to behold. A few well-placed plants in a small office can make the room look very comfortable and luxurious, even if the only furniture is a steel desk and chair. Hanging plants are marvellous for covering a scene that's not to your taste, such as old Venetian blinds or a poor view. Most offices are lit with fluorescent lights, and although office light is usually up to the basic minimum required for plant growth, choose plants that are easy to look after and that can exist in low light. Try to have fairly large pots, preferably plastic ones because they hold water for longer; after all, in an office we are concerned mainly with working, not with watering plants. Good employees in your office are Scheffleras, any type of Dracaena, Rubber Trees, Grape Ivy, Spider Plants, and Fatsias. And one further point: allow only *one* person to water the plants in your office—preferably you—and slap the fingers of anyone you see using a planter as a receptacle for old coffee grounds and cigarette butts.

Lastly, when you're all set to be your own designer, take courage—follow your own instincts! There's always the old dilemma: 'Should I change my plants to match the room, or should I change the room to match my plants?' All the suggestions I've made in this chapter are excellent (of course!), but who am *I* to tell *you* what good design is? I like pastel colours and greys; you may like bright, shimmering colours. I like Art Deco and plain casual furniture—you may like gilt and Bokharas. It always makes me a little sad when I meet people who just aren't sure what is 'right'. Anything that pleases you is definitely right—for you. If you get an idea, no matter how kooky, try it; for all we know, you have better ideas than anyone else.

Schefflera

8

Best Friends

I'm off to the greenhouse again—I just can't keep away!
There's so much to look at: all those colourful green mar-
vels, and sometimes, among them, the rare and exciting
newcomers that appear every so often in a special shipment
from some exotic land. I never know what unusual plant I'll
find.

What I mean by 'unusual' is any plant other than the
ordinary stock plants that are carried by every greenhouse
I've ever gone to. Now don't get me wrong, I haven't anything against our more common plants—it's only that I
know them so well. They're like dear old friends. Maybe I
know my old friends so well that I almost take them for
granted (the novelty of a new affair is attractive in itself),
but you may not have met some of these plants yet, so let
me introduce you to a few of them. 'Jane and Bill, I'd like
you to meet Schefflera and Areca.'

Schefflera

Scheffleras are probably the most popular of the large house
plants, with humans and red spiders alike. The big dark-

green multi-fingered branches of the Schefflera can be seen peeking out of the windows of stores, homes, and offices in every city in North America. Even Dent Canada, the publishers of this book, display a good old Schefflera in their lobby. There are a number of favourite tricks Scheffleras like to pull on their owners. An over-watered Schefflera goes black at the ends of the leaves or, worse still, on the stalk. A black tip can be cut off without much agony, but a black stalk means death to every part of the plant above the black area. Keep your Schefflera on the dry side; the soil in a 12-inch pot should feel dry down to at least three-quarters of an inch before you rewater it. I have met very few Scheffleras that didn't have red spiders, so check yours carefully before you buy it and keep an eye open for them at all times. Scheffleras don't need a great deal of light (either indirect or moderate light is best, though they can manage even in poor light), but they have a tendency to drop their lower leaves, and to discourage them from doing that you should make sure the light shines on the bottom of the plant as well as on the top.

Are you coming to the conclusion that Sheffleras are difficult? Nothing could be further from the truth. They are very hardy, can stand a fair amount of abuse, and even when they become dilapidated (that's 'tatty') they are well able to regrow to their former beauty in no time at all.

Palms: *Areca* **and** *Erumpens*

These are not the only palms in existence, but they are by far the best known. The Erumpens Palm is a bamboo type; it's the right size to fit into small areas, yet still create a big-plant effect. Aside from red spiders, which plague almost everything, this plant is all but worry free. Keep it lightly moist. If it's in a 12-inch pot, allow the soil to feel dry to about half an inch down. Like our friend the Schefflera, Erumpens likes to grow from the top, so make sure the bottom of the plant is well lit and it won't get leggy. Erumpens prefers indirect to moderate light.

The Areca Palm is the spreading, elegant, Victorian-type palm. I really like Areca Palms, they are so striking and graceful—just lovely. It's not a worry-free plant, however: it's very fussy about humidity. Hot, dry, winter conditions cause many brown leaf-tips. You know that all palms enjoy being misted—the Areca *insists* on it. Forget to mist, and your Areca will punish you for it. The plant's watering and light needs are the same as for the Erumpens; fortunately Arecas are not so fussy as their cousins about light on their lower reaches, because they always spring up from the bottom, anyway. The Achilles' heel of Areca Palms is scale. Check the lower part of the plant and the undersides of fronds for white or brown dots. Sometimes over-enthusiastic greenhouse men plant Areca Palms too low in the soil, inadvertently causing a condition known as crown rot. The stems end in elongated onion shapes clustered at the bottom of the plant. When properly planted, the entire onion shape should be visible; if soil covers any part of the crown, clear away the excess. You will know you have crown rot if the stalks of the fronds, which have been dying dramatically, can easily be tweaked from their bases by a single pull. If you examine the end of a stalk, you'll see it looks mouldy and decayed.

... *left, Erumpens Palm*   ... *right, Areca Palm*

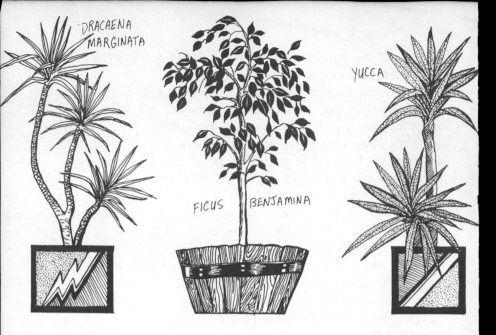

DRACAENA MARGINATA

FICUS BENJAMINA

YUCCA

The Dracaena Family

After Scheffleras, Dracaenas are probably the most popular of the large house plants: Madame Marginata is the most courted of all her sisters. Dracaenas are stalk plants, growing on long, solid trunks from which clumps of spiky leaves protrude. Most Dracaenas regularly lose their lower leaves, but because you probably bought the plant for its different-looking bare bottom, this is no great tragedy. Dracaenas are tough; they always seem to do better when slightly neglected rather than coddled. Keep the soil on the dry side, allowing it to dry out to at least three-quarters of an inch down in a 12-inch pot. As for light, Dracaenas will stand anything from bright indirect to poor light. If a Dracaena, especially a Marginata, is not turned regularly, the whole top of the plant will bend over and grow parallel to the floor towards the light. A Marginata that hasn't been turned for about a year needs everything but flying buttresses to keep it from falling over. As usual, red spiders have eyes for Dracaenas (what *don't* they like?), and mealybugs also seem to find them very tasty.

Ficus benjamina

A Benjamina is a real fuss budget. This highly-strung, nervous little plant seems to have only one thing going for it—its beauty, and is it beautiful! Some people think that if they buy a big hulk of a Benjamina it won't be as delicate as a smaller one; unfortunately, no matter how big a Benjamina is, he is still a big sissie. (I'm sure a 3-inch cutting of Grape Ivy could get away with kicking sand in the face of a 20-foot Benjamina.) Benjaminas don't like draughts, they hate too much light, loathe too little light, have fits if they get too dry, and sulk if they are kept too moist. The only thing I'm positive a Benjamina does like is to drop leaves. I hate to paint such a bad picture of our pretty friend with the birch-tree elegance, but it's only too true. I not only suggest, I *implore* you not to buy a Benjamina until you feel confident about growing house plants. We've lost more potential indoor gardeners to something safe, like stamp collecting, because they started their gardening careers with a Benjamina. If you own one, or feel ready, willing, and able enough to try owning one, keep the soil lightly moist. It should dry down to only about half an inch in a 12-inch pot. Keep your temperamental companion in bright diffused or moderate light, and in a draught-free area, and keep the humidity up. Benjaminas are fresh, cheerful-looking house plants; once you get one to settle in to your home you'll find it a real blessing.

Yucca

After all my complaints about Benjaminas, perhaps it's about time I found a plant to praise. Thank heaven for Yuccas. Yuccas are hardy, uncomplaining, and interesting. They are plants growing on long stalks, like Dracaenas, with their long, thick poles supporting sharp, pointed grey-green leaves. I'm sure there must be some bug that likes to chew on Yuccas, but of all the hundreds I have seen in my travels, I have yet to find one with even a minor infestation of anything. Unless the plant is kept in a closet with the door shut, or left standing outside with snow on its leaves, the something that's gone wrong with a Yucca is usually that it's simply getting too much water. Yes, I do find lots of over-watered ones. Yuccas naturally lose their lower leaves in the course of time, so as long as the 'head' stays the same size, don't worry; but if the head decreases and looks stunted, it's time for you to fret and fidget. Yucca likes anything from direct sunlight to poor light, performing best in a spot that receives either bright or diffused bright sunlight. Water it only when the soil is dry down to at least 2 inches in a 12-inch pot.

Rubber Tree   (*Ficus elastica*)

I saw a photograph, taken by a friend of a friend, of a Rubber Tree in Tahiti. The photographer, his wife, two other friends, and their car, were all standing under only one part of it. He had taken the picture because he owned a 3-foot-high, nine-leaved version of the same tree, and, obviously, visions of the future grandeur of his own prize had spurred him on. What he didn't know is that most Rubber Trees are the closest approach to plastic plants imaginable. I've heard countless clients complain that their three-year-old hasn't yet grown a new leaf. The plant hasn't dropped any, mind you, but grow—well, that's another story. For these unfortunate people I have but one piece of advice: be patient. A Rubber Tree will put up with almost no light, but it will grow best in indirect or moderate light. Although not a showy plant, it certainly is a sturdy one. Rubber Trees don't like to be watered too much, especially when they are not growing. Water them whenever the soil is dry from about half to three-quarters of an inch down in an 8-inch pot. Rubber Trees show discontent by dropping their lower leaves, which they usually do when they think they're being given either too much or too little water.

Philodendron

Philodendrons! Your grandmother had one, your dentist has one, your barber, your neighbour—it seems everyone has one. I often wonder when some smart young Philly will put on shoes and overcoat and start living outside: if one did that, Philodendrons would quickly take over the country from coast to coast. The plant with heart-shaped leaves—I'm sure we all know it—has the grand title *Philodendron oxycardium (cordatum)*. But don't let its name scare you: the plant will grow you out of house and home with only token care and light. His big brother, the Split-leaf Philodendron, is also extremely hardy, doesn't like intense light, but must be in bright indirect light if you want the leaves to 'split'. I personally much prefer the Philodendron Selloum, which has large, ruffled, multi-fingered leaves elevated on long fleshy stalks that rise up out of the pot with great presence. No Philodendron likes direct sunlight, or soggy socks; always let the soil dry out to at least three-quarters of an inch down in a 12-inch pot. Though common, and somewhat uninspired looking, I must admit that Philodendrons are a godsend for a spot that only receives very little light.

RUBBER TREE   PHILODENDRON

Grape Ivy

Now here's a good-looking plant which, in a poorly lit spot, will perform every bit as well as a Philodendron, and is hardy enough to ignore the attacks of even the most persistent of the infamous bugs. I've seen Grape Ivy, white with mealybugs, gaily sending out new shoots as if nothing was wrong. Grape Ivies are also the pincher's dream come true; pinch a growing point on this plant and it will branch out obediently. Grow Grape Ivy in anything from indirect to poor light, but keep it out of the sun, please. Water liberally, then allow it to dry out to about an inch down in a 6-inch pot. Whenever you repot your Grape Ivy, try to remember that it really appreciates peat moss.

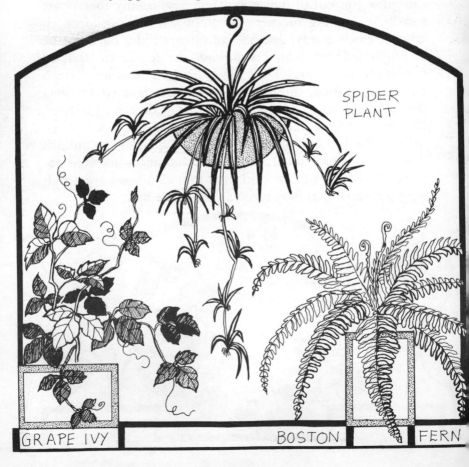

SPIDER PLANT

GRAPE IVY   BOSTON   FERN

Spider Plant   (*Chlorophytum*)

Some people love Spider Plants, others hate them with passion. I can never see exactly what there is to loathe about a green and white plant that produces little plants as babies, but some people actually do feel very strongly about them. 'I wouldn't have a Spider Plant in *my* house if . . . if you paid me!' Assuming that you're not a hater of Spider Plants, I'll tell you a bit about them.

The hardiest Spider Plants are the all-green kind. These will grow big and produce lots of long arms that flower and become plants in their own right in half the light needed for the variegated type. The surest way to grow a green and white (variegated) Spider Plant is to grow one from a baby given you by a friend, since fully grown hothouse Spiders usually have not been acclimatized properly, and because of that many of their leaves will suffer from brown tips for the first few weeks. Both these types of Spiders like to stay dry to about half to three-quarters of an inch down between waterings in, say, a 10-inch hanging pot. They like morning sun or bright diffused light, though the all-green variety will accept poorer light. Contrary to the opinions expressed in a number of plant books, I have yet to find a red spider on a Spider Plant. What I do find is scale, lots of scale; so watch for it when you're buying yours.

Boston Fern   (*Nephrolepsis exaltata bostoniensis*)

On my recent trip to England, I saw ferns that would make you cry: big, bushy, green ferns without even a trace of a brown tip anywhere. In Canada, I see brown tips on every frond—and yellow centres, too, and growth that is pale and small. What have the English got that we haven't? Could it be anything to do with those 600-year-old lawns? Maybe, but in proud defence of my fellow countrymen, I must state strongly that it's not *us*, it's our hot dry air. We Canadians usually do pretty well with our ferns in the summer but, come winter, instead of our ferns going to sleep for a nice few months of dormancy like all good English ferns, ours crisp up and die. Ferns like to stay lightly moist, so you should allow only the surface of the soil to feel dry; then rewater. Fish fertilizer twice a month from March to November keeps them green and growing. And mist, mist, mist. In the winter, if you can keep them cool (44-55°F; 4-13°C), water them less and let them recuperate from all their energetic summer growing.

Wandering Jew   (*Tradescantia* or *Zebrina*)

This has to be one of the only plants I know that will really grow with a vengeance in direct sunlight or at the bottom of a deep dark mineshaft. Most plants that do well in the brightest sun die in poor light, and those that get along in poor light perish in the sun—but not Wandering Jew! My first Wandering Jew I rescued one chilly November; it was half-submerged in an unspeakably filthy pool of water in an abandoned freezer. These odds against survival meant nothing to that plant: it soon looked like a million dollars!

The plants come in all manner of leaf colours and patterns. If you find that your once purple-and-green plant is now only green, and you don't mind, fine; it will still grow. But if you want the colour back, you'll have to put it in stronger light. Wandering Jews like a thorough drenching and then to dry out; allow the soil to dry half an inch down in a 6-inch pot.

English Ivy   (*Hedera helix*)

I have seen an English Ivy, planted in a 4-inch pot, which had grown, over the years, one branch. This branch travelled across the windowsill, up the window, along the ceiling to the next window, and then around that window twice. I did pat this client on the head for her good work; then I mentioned, of course, the need for repotting, and preached on the potential of pinching. An unpinched Ivy will grow one or two branches—forever. Up to this point I have been talking about healthy Ivies; sadly enough, there are only a few of them around, the rest all have red spiders. Not one Ivy should enter your home without the following: first, a thorough inspection; second, a good spraying for red spider; third, a careful quarantine; and, finally, another spraying for red spider. Yes, they sound like pretty strong measures for just one little plant, but I'll never forget the words of a greenhouse man I know and respect, when he said, 'Once I get rid of these Ivies, that's it! No more Ivies; those spiders are driving me crazy!'

Ivies like to be on the cool side, if and when possible, and to stay lightly moist. Allow the soil in a 6-inch pot to dry down to about half an inch before rewatering. Ivies like anything from bright indirect to poor light, and will grow where most plants would suffer. But remember, don't forget to pinch.

ENGLISH
IVY

Wandering
Jew

... *left, Jade Plant;
centre, 'Asparagus
sprengeri'; right,
'Asparagus plumosus'*

Jade Plant   (*Crassula*)

The mistake people make when they are caring for a Jade
plant is in the watering: they mist the plant, put it in good
light, then water it all wrong. There are two schools of
thought (or non-thought, perhaps) about Jades and how to
water them. One group thinks that these plants are a type of
desert cactus: these people like to wait three weeks to a
month before they dribble a minute ration of water into the
plant's pot. Group number two thinks that this plant is one
and the same as all other house plants, and doles out a
generous portion of water every other day. A few months
after the people in the first group have carefully provided
desert conditions, their Jade is shrivelling like a prune. The
second group's Jade, watered so frequently, usually topples
out of its pot one day as the owner is admiring it. If it
weren't for improper watering, every Jade that was ever
planted would probably still be alive today.

Because Jade plants are semi-succulent, the amount of
water you give them should be exactly halfway between the
amount you would give cacti and the amount needed by the
average house plant. Water a Jade only when the soil has
dried halfway down the depth of the pot, but don't let it dry
out completely. The best way to tell when a Jade needs
water is to feel the leaves; when they begin to feel very

slightly soft, a little bit less firm than usual, rewater. Jades always drop some of their leaves in the winter, so don't be concerned, it will grow them all back, plus more, in the spring. Jade trees like bright moderate light, but won't stand constant direct sunlight or poor light.

Asparagus

One of my very favourite plants is my Asparagus. There are two types that are commonly sold as house plants: *Asparagus sprengeri*, which produces cascading waterfalls of bright-green fronds with needle-like leaves, and *Asparagus plumosus*, producing erect dark-green feathery fronds—these are the fern-like fronds that are usually sold with a single rose. I have both kinds of Asparagus, but it's my big old grandfather-of-them-all Sprengeri that I love the most. He perches 'way up in my skylight, and seems to pour out of his pot down into the kitchen. He flowers in late summer: dainty little yellowish-white flowers. Attractive, but they do not smell nice—in fact, their smell reminds me of old cheese or rancid butter. But after the weird odours come bright little red berries that are worth waiting for.

Asparagus sprengeri just love bright light, but will not do well in poor light. I water my big Asparagus every second day, giving him about half a quart of water; two days later the soil is always dry again. Never let an Asparagus dry out. Check it every two days if it's in a large pot, every day if it's in a small pot. Asparagus in direct sun even for part of the day usually needs to be watered once a day, especially if it's in a terra cotta pot. One final note about the Sprengeri: they are very unwilling to leave their old pots—their thick, fleshy, white roots seem to have muscles! To repot your plant, you may have to break the pot or, if its roots are tangled up with the roots of other plants in a planter, you may have to do some hacking and tearing. If so, you will lose a few fronds— but not to worry; Sprengeri have great staying power.

9

Those Exotic Visitors from Faraway Places

'What's that? Oh, that's a *Ficus rubiginosa variegata*. Those things grow like weeds! Why, you hardly need to look at them and they grow.' The man in charge of the green plants who made that statement would probably be more successful as a used-car salesman. Every now and again, a truly exotic-looking specimen shows up, sitting among the Grape Ivies and Scheffleras in your plant store. Rare it may be, and exotic; but easy to care for—now that is definitely another story. Have you ever wondered why your local plant emporium doesn't carry plants such as Banana Trees, Orchids, Jasmine, and other fabulous-sounding creations? The reason is really quite simple: most of the plants we know as 'rare' are rare because they are very difficult, if not impossible, to grow as house plants. And then, more often than not, the disillusioned new owner of a rarity swiftly returns it, crying out that he or she was sold a lemon. Some exotic beauties need incredibly high humidity, others need extremely cool places to be happy in. Whatever they need, it's usually something you cannot supply in your home without considerable overwork or discomfort to yourself.

Much as I like plants, I have always felt strongly that it

makes good sense to adhere to this simple rule of gardening: you ought to rule over and enjoy your plants, they shouldn't rule over you. 'I'm sorry, Fred, I can't come out tonight; I have to stay home and mist my Banana Tree.' Whatever you do, please don't let your plants bully you around; make *them* fit into *your* system, or show them the door. There is nothing worse than a bunch of spoiled-brat plants, always asking for something more.

There are many occasions in our lives when we start a new venture and, if we like it, we try to advance and progress. The day will come when every plant you own is growing well, and you will start to look for greener pastures. Luckily for us, there are a few exotic lovelies that, with the proper respect, will grow like weeds. Interested? Good. Here are a few of my favourites—plants that will look 'different' and will grow for the watchful gardener.

String of Hearts (*Ceropegia woodii*)

I searched high and low for this plant, but now I finally have one. Ceropegia has small heart-shaped leaves, a delicate grey-green in colour, which grow on long, thin, hanging stems resembling strings. At various points grow flowers that look like miniature gourds. Everything about the plant is small and refined—Ceropegia always reminds me of dainty Victorian lace work. For the life of me, I can't figure out why this plant is so rare. It's beautiful and, as far as I can tell, as strong as a bull. It laughs at dry air, and doesn't complain a bit if you are late in watering it—in fact it *likes* to stay a little on the dry side. Unless you have a monster, you will probably have it in a small pot; you should allow a 4-inch pot to dry from about half to three-quarters of an inch down before rewatering. The happiest Ceropegias are in bright diffused to moderate light. This is truly a plant that will win friends and influence people.

Chenille Plant (*Acalypha*)

Long, red, fuzzy tails hanging down from all over every twig not only look exotic, they look unreal. He who thought up Acalyphas sure was using His thinking cap and heavenly magic markers that day! 'Hey, I want another drink!' Acalyphas love water. A dry one is a sad sight, all the leaves just hanging limply from the branches. Keep the soil evenly moist; allow the surface (only the surface) to dry, then rewater. These plants don't like the dark, and hate strong sunlight; indirect, moderate light is best for them. Acalyphas have a remarkable growing cycle. In the spring, they burst out with hundreds of growing points; then, in a month or so, all you can see are their broad green leaves poking out in every direction. By midsummer the red-hot cattails appear, and, as they grow, the plant begins to lose all its lower leaves. The end result is a crown of big green leaves, and a fabulous circular display of cattails. Then in winter, one by one, off come the tails. Acalypha is another plant that is so easy to care for and yet is rarely available. Curious indeed.

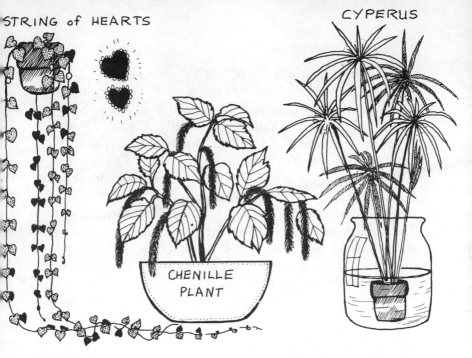

STRING of HEARTS

CYPERUS

CHENILLE
PLANT

Cyperus

Thank God for small miracles: Cyperus is now being sold more frequently than it used to be. *Cyperus alternifolius* is a smaller version of the bulrushes among which Moses was found floating in a basket, when he was a baby. It's a river plant, and is one of the few plants I know that actually like to stand in water. One of my clients made an indoor gold-fish pond; for decoration she sank three pots of Cyperus right in the pond, and they're really flourishing. If you are the type of person who likes to see a plant grow right before your eyes, Cyperus is the plant for you! A new shoot will rise 1, 2, even 5 or 6 feet into the air on a clean, leafless stalk, then with a flourish the arrowhead pops open, and out comes a circular fan of long slim leaves. Keep your Cyperus in bright indirect light if you want sturdy growth, though don't despair even if you can't give it bright light, for I've come across them thriving in poor light, too.

Aralia

I fully realize that our friends in the Aralia family are far from rare, but because most of them exhibit impossible temperaments I have included them in this chapter. Before I begin on the difficult side of the family, I want to tell you about my sweetheart, the Fatsia. This beautiful foliage plant with the unfortunate name is hardy, full, and absolutely lovable. Fatsias have fresh-looking, dark-green leaves that resemble maple leaves. Usually sold as 6-inch house plants, they can grow very tall. They require lots of water, wilting dramatically when dry. Allow the soil to dry to a quarter of an inch down in a 6-inch pot. A big feature of a Fatsia is that it will grow even in the poorest light. Keep it in any light from bright diffused to poor.

If Fatsia is the least temperamental of the Aralias, its relative, *Dizygotheca elegantissima*, is as difficult to care for as its name is to pronounce. But Elegantissimas are exactly what their fancy name implies: very elegant. Tall brown stems support hundreds of multi-fingered shiny leaves with lacy edges, in the most beautiful reddish-green colour. That description was of a healthy Elegantissima, and unfortunately healthy ones aren't as common as you might expect. I think an Elegantissima should have two names: its real name would last it from the day it's born to the day it enters your home; then its name should change (as the plant always does) to a new one: 'Dropus lotsaleafus'. I have three Elegantissimas (or is it four?) that have been struggling for life ever since they were pronounced dead—in other words, unwanted—by a client. They're growing, but life isn't easy for them—or for me! Keep your Elegantissima slightly moist, allow the soil to dry half an inch down in a 12-inch pot; don't ever let it dry out completely, or keep it too wet. Mist it a hundred times a day in winter if possible, keep it in bright diffused to moderate light—and good luck!

The last of the Aralias I'm going to mention is the *Aralia polyscias*. There are a number of different leaf shapes and hues to choose from, but all the plants usually produce delicate ruffled leaves that look similar to fat carrot leaves. These pretty green friends are not as easy to care for as a Fatsia nor as difficult as an Elegantissima, but look after them as carefully as you would an Elegantissima and I promise you will have much better results.

Episcia

Sitting not 5 feet away from me at this moment is my 'Silver Sheen' Episcia, merrily blooming away. Episcias really love to bloom, and they usually do it during the winter months. They are incredibly colourful; my Silver Sheen has a white-green leaf with brownish-purple edges and mauve undersides. Couple that with clusters of little orange-red, trumpet-shaped flowers, and you'll have a picture of my pride and joy. No matter how hard the wind blows outside in the winter, this vision will cheer you up. Episcias like to dry out between waterings—to about half to three-quarters of an inch down in an 8-inch pot—and enjoy indirect to moderate light and even some sun. One more nice thing about Episcias: like Spider Plants, they also have babies. A happy Episcia will produce them on the ends of furry arms, making this plant a natural for hanging.

FATSIA

EPISCIA

Leaf of
DIZYGOTHECA
ELEGANTISSIMA

Calathea

Some people collect clocks, others like rare coins or books; I collect Calatheas. In the six months I've been collecting I have now got four varieties of them, but considering that I know of twenty types I want altogether, I guess I still have a long way to go before I complete my collection. Calatheas are not easily come by: it seems you have to all but stand on a dingy, wet street corner and wait for your Calathea contact to get one for you. If Episcias are colourful, Calatheas are dazzling—the top of the leaf looks like a piece of hand-painted fine-quality china. The face of the leaf is 'painted' in bold strokes of dark green or grey, with finely drawn line designs etched around them. The back of the leaf is almost an exact negative of the front, in mauve or pink matte, while the front is glossy and shiny. Calatheas are similar to the Prayer Plant (*Maranta erythroneura*), but instead of growing long trailing branches that ultimately have to be cut, Calatheas spring upright from the soil, producing a thicket of stems, so that the plant becomes fuller and fuller. They like to be kept moderately moist (allow the soil to dry half an inch down in a 6-inch pot) and enjoy medium brightness of light. By the way, if you see one for sale, call me!

Lithops

Lithops are called the 'Living Stone' Plant, because each one really looks like a little pebble. They are guaranteed to bring tears to the eyes of even the hardest of hearts, for these tiny cacti, without prickles, look so small and defenceless that you instantly get the urge to declare you will protect them forever. Caring for Lithops is incredibly easy: water them whenever the soil they are in is totally dry, and keep them in bright light or sun. If you are really good to them, they will not only grow but produce beautiful little daisy-like flowers for you.

Lithops

Jasmine

Believe it or not, this heavily scented, profusely flowering plant is not the least bit difficult to grow. All you need is bright light and a cool room; a sunroom or glass-roofed patio is excellent. If you like the scene of Jasmine in your tea, imagine it filling your home! The perfume from even a modest-sized Jasmine plant can become overpowering, though; in the same way you almost get a headache from sitting next to a young girl who has overdone it with borrowed perfume, a lot of Jasmine blooming in a small room can almost do you in. But what a way to go—perfumed to death by Jasmine. Besides smelling nice, the flowers are really pretty. They're small in size, but what the Jasmine flower loses in size it definitely gains in numbers. I have a Jasmine about 2 feet 6 inches high and a foot wide. Once when it was blooming I decided to count the flowers—silly, I know, but I was proud of my plant and wanted to find out just how many blooms it could produce. I gave up counting when I got to the middle sixties and hadn't even covered all the plant. If you like scented flowers, Jasmine is the plant for you. Jasmine likes very bright light best, but will grow in moderate light. Keep it slightly moist; allow the soil to dry down to about half or three-quarters of an inch in a 12-inch pot.

Kangaroo Vine (*Cissus antarctica*)

Kangaroo Vine is a blood relative of the Grape Ivy; like the Grape Ivy it is a vine and really quite hardy. Its winning points are great big lime-green leaves with jagged edges. Try as I might, I have never been able to figure out why it's called Kangaroo Vine; it doesn't bounce, have big legs or a pocket, yet it must have got the name somewhere. Maybe one of its first indoor admirers forgot to look at his new plant for a while and then discovered that it had grown by leaps and bounds. Kangaroo Vines do not like to be kept too wet; if they are, the leaves will turn grey and dry to a crisp. I know that this information is directly opposed to what I have told you are the symptoms of over-watering—now you know why my book has thousands of 'most's and 'usually's in it: there is always one plant that *has* to be different. Unlike Grape Ivy, Kangaroo Vines do not enjoy darkish places, and although they will survive in low light, they need bright indirect light if they are to thrive.

Flowering Maple (*Abutilon*)

This plant has to be the most delicate-*looking* piece of greenery I have mentioned so far. Thin branches and trunk support floppy maple-like leaves that are either green or spotted with white and yellow. To top that, it has big tangerine-coloured bell-shaped flowers that hang down at the end

of a little limp neck from a joint on the stem. Flowering Maple gives you the impression that, if you touched it, it would simply fall apart. Nothing could be further from the truth; although it is not as tough as a Philodendron or Grape Ivy, it certainly could stand up to the biggest Benjamina or Elegantissima. It's usually very difficult to find a plant that looks delicate but isn't—as far as care is concerned. Abutilon fills that bill perfectly. Water it whenever the soil is dry to about half an inch down in a 6-inch pot, and keep your plant in bright diffused to moderate light.

So there's your selection of 'rare' plants! All the ones I have mentioned can be tracked down: the fact that I have four varieties of Calathea proves this. You may have rather a job getting them, but when you do, you are entitled to feel really proud of them when they grow and blossom for you in your home.

111

10

The Magic Combination —Plants and People

As you may have noticed, throughout this book I have been dwelling at some length on the idea that you shouldn't ever give up on a plant before you are certain it is completely dead. In this day of plastic disposable everything, I insist that there should be at least one aspect of life that requires people to use their own talents and abilities for best results. I can never understand why some people will do everything in their power to save the life of their sick dog or cat, but let two leaves fall off one of their plant showpieces, and it is immediately declared undesirable and flung into the trash can. Plants are not pieces of furniture, like couches or cushions, to be dusted, fluffed up, and re-covered every other year: plants are living, growing things—absolutely marvellous things.

You realize, of course, that without plants we wouldn't be able to drive our cars, heat our homes, or, for that matter, build them—in fact, I think, without plants we couldn't exist. Even though we might be able to survive somehow, plants, on the other hand, could get along easily enough without *us*. Have you ever imagined how difficult it would be for science to produce raw energy in safe, storable containers from nothing else but the sun, the air, and the soil? Not only produce it, but produce it without polluting the environment with gases, waste, and radiation. If such a project were to be set before our men of science, it would take them years to develop a 'plant' that could do the job effectively, and I'm sure this factory would be large and complex, and its product expensive. Since the dawn of Earth, the smallest plant in the prehistoric jungle has been turning out just such a product without a second thought, taking nourishing ingredients from the soil, adding water and air, mixing the whole brew with sunlight, and presto!—energy to be safely stored away in containers in the shape of leaves, stems, and roots. Put these containers under heat and pressure and you get coal; let them rot and store them for a long time, and you get petroleum; or simply dry them out and burn them right now, if you prefer. All the plants you're growing today could be the coal and oil of the future; think of it—your Spider Plant could be a source of energy for future relations!

This whole sermon has brought me to another aspect of plants that I must preach about. Currently there are a number of people who believe that if you sing, talk, or do rain dances, your plants will flourish all the better. If you show anger or, worse still, have a domestic quarrel with your mate, your plant will react by wilting, losing its leaves, or just plain dropping dead from a plant heart attack. Leave

plants are not pieces of furniture ······

LIFETIME GUARANTEE
ACME PLANT Co.
WRINKLE RESISTANT
SKUFF PROOF
NEEDS NO PRUNING
EASY TO ASSEMBLE
SUITABLE FOR FRAMING
FOLDS INTO HANDY CARD TABLE
DRY CLEAN ONLY

home, and your plants will miss you—the list goes on and on. If this trend continues, I can imagine the plant books of the future giving advice like this: 'When you are entering a plant store to buy a prospective new friend, put on a friendly face, think nice thoughts, and, whatever you do, *don't* act superior, plants absolutely hate that! Tickle the little fellow gently under a leaf, and ask him if he likes you enough to go home with you. If he doesn't drop a leaf, good —you've made it to first base with him. Next, always remember to say "please" and "thank you" when you ask for or receive any gifts from your plant, such as flowers. Never put on a record or turn on the TV without first asking your plant's permission; if he doesn't want to hear anything, *don't ever* lose your temper and turn on the sound anyway!'

Plants are supposed to like music. But not just ordinary music—our plants are supposed to like only the most formal classical music. Why they are imagined to be so selective I cannot for the life of me guess. Isn't it possible that there are some excitable young-hearted plants who really love to move to the beat of 'disco' music, or groove on psychedelic sounds? Myself, I'm a young man; and although I do have

many classical records, the part of my collection I most enjoy, and the largest part, is the loud and flashy stuff that's supposed to curl the leaves of any self-respecting plant. Funny, I don't understand why my plants haven't passed out en masse as yet. One other thing distresses me about all this business of communicating with plants: if it *is* true that plants should have music, love, and conversation in order to grow, what about all those poor, lonely, deprived plants growing out there in the country with only bird song for music? All those evergreen trees crying themselves to sleep every night, those hundreds of despondent deciduous trees, all straining their leaves in vain to hear just one bar of Bacharach or Beethoven. Perhaps it's their solitude that makes them grow so well. To put it bluntly: until someone — a respectable university, perhaps — can prove to me that this particular kind of attention will make my plants grow better, I will neither believe in any of it nor practise it. I still think that no matter how much you talk to your plant, or sing and dance for it, if you don't water it right and give it the best conditions, that plant is going to do poorly.

Have you ever wondered why everybody seems to have gone crazy about plants in the last few years? There are plenty of reasons for the Great Plant Boom, plus a few more I may forget to mention or haven't thought of, but all of them have something to do with our environment. Living twenty-five floors in the air in a concrete building with a view of houses, buildings, and factories for as far as the eye can see is definitely the strongest reason. We are not the first generation of people to live in large, congested cities (for centuries there have been big cities) but we are probably the first to realize that in a short time there may be nothing but one big city stretching all around the world. The day is not far off when a person will be from the 'little town' of Brantford, Corner Brook, or Medicine Hat — population of each centre 2,000,000. I think urban sprawl scares people — it certainly scares me! When the whole world has been divided up into streets, office towers, and shopping plazas, we shall have to go to the Zoo not only to see the nearly extinct Polar bears but also the nearly extinct pine trees. It's getting harder and harder to find untouched wilderness. My reaction to these horrifying contemplations was to fill my house with plants, and I think I'm by no means the only one who's done that.

There is something in each one of us that makes us feel the need for a dependent to give our lives more meaning. All of us—especially perhaps single people, couples who have no children, or those whose children have flown the nest—seem to need something to care for. Pets are one answer, but as most apartments don't allow them, plants fill the bill admirably. The last and probably the strongest reason for the plant boom is that plants are in fashion right now. Pick up any 'trendy' design magazine, visit any new office, shopping plaza, or restaurant, and you will see plants everywhere. But why? Why did all the designers suddenly start to use live plants when they created new offices, plazas, and homes? For the very simple reason, I feel, that as design became more functional and uncluttered it also became somewhat colder in atmosphere—so cold, in fact, that it seems certain that almost any of today's offices and lobbies would intimidate anyone, unless they were made a little more inviting with the use of natural greenery. The dream of the future in the days of Buck Rogers—the 1920s and 30s —was of a world in which everything was made and controlled by man. Now that we seem to be approaching this dream, it has changed, most of us are thankful to realize, to a dream of living in harmony with ourselves and nature.

So that's the psychological and sociological aspect of plants, as seen by me! Now for a little talk on the idiosyncrasies of people—those of people who have impressed me with their ways of caring for plants. First, the men. I've found men really fun to watch and to talk to whenever I am making a house call. Men, especially doctors, lawyers, and businessmen, usually pretend not to be at all interested in the fate of their particular plant (they are always a little

embarrassed and amused by the idea of a visiting plant doctor), but they always end up asking questions and showing the greatest interest in all the proceedings. A typical lawyer, perhaps, who has a dying plant in his office, is always 'busy' with papers or the phone when his secretary and I enter to inspect the patient. After I have been there for a minute or two he will always ask a few 'I don't know anything about plants, but...' questions; then after the 'but' follows a barrage of very specific enquiries, all showing that he may not 'know' about plants but he sure has a lot of ideas. One client of mine is a businessman who owns a fairly large company with a number of employees. After spending the day with his workers, for whom he has to pretend to be a combination of Einstein and Ghengis Khan, he likes to come home, sit among his plants, and relax. The large number of plants there are all doing very well. He's content to allow his wife to water and mist 'his' plants—until one is doing poorly. Whenever one of 'his' becomes sick, he becomes a man of action, reserving the complete nursing of the sick one for himself, and threatening with harsh punishments anyone who even dares to touch it until it has completely recovered.

Women seem to be split into two groups. One group is always in abject terror that its brood of green friends are all going to die; the other insists that its plants shape up and grow. The ladies in the first group are usually great with plants, but haven't realized it yet. How many times have I gone to a house where the plants are gleamingly clean, bushy, and robust, but their hand-wringing owner, completely lacking in self-confidence, is certain that just because her plants all *look* so fit, they're going to die! If you feel you may be one of this group, I suggest you walk through your home, stick your tongue out at each and every plant you own, and say, 'Just try and die, and see what happens! Ha! I won't let you!' (This won't do anything for—or against—your plants, but it might help *you*.)

Those in the second group are really fun. Every morning

they begin a busy day by sending the kids off to school, feeding the dog, the cat, and the husband, then they themselves either rush off to work or begin to clean the house, do the laundry, and work, work, work. They flash through the house, watering, pinching, and checking their plants in what seems to be only seconds, almost daring any of them to get out of line, and thinking, 'Huh! We'll see about that!' In the same way they may suspect that their son is going to come down with a cold (by the way he asked to watch one more programme on TV before bed last night), they are quick to spot any trouble that may have affected their plants. It's how they react to trouble that's wonderful: they inspect, diagnose, and treat, in seconds; they never worry about the outcome, and usually they are right.

I'm sure you never expected to be hit with such a short but thought-provoking sermonette (though some might call it lengthy and possibly sleep-inducing) when you began to read this chapter, but if there is one thing that I, Brian Murphy the Plant Doctor, would like to do, it's to get people not only to like plants but to *love* them.

Bibliography

Cruso, Thalassa, *Making Things Grow* (New York: Knopf, 1970) 288 pp.; a most enjoyable book, perfect for the beginner.

Elbert, George A., *The Indoor Light Gardening Book* (New York: Crown Publishers, 1973) 256 pp.

Evans, Charles M. and Pliner, Roberta L., *Rx for Ailing Houseplants* (New York: Random House, 1974) 112 pp., paperback; all the bugs and diseases.

Fitch, Charles M., *The Complete Book of Houseplants* (New York: Hawthorn Books, 1972) 320 pp.; highly recommended.

Graf, Alfred B., *Exotica*, Series 3, 7th edition (New Jersey: Roehrs, 1974) 1834 pp.; a manual of house plants; 4,200 black-and-white illustrations; very detailed and informative.

Herwig, Rob, *128 Houseplants You Can Grow* (New York: Collier Macmillan, 1972) 64 pp., paperback; colour photographs of all the plants that are described; information on how to care for each plant; straightforward and easy to use.

Herwig, Rob, *128 More Houseplants You Can Grow* (New York: Collier Macmillan, 1974) 64 pp., paperback; a continuation of *128 Houseplants You Can Grow*.

Kranz, Frederick H. and Kranz, Jacqueline L., *Gardening Indoors Under Lights* (New York: Lancer Books, 1971) 256 pp., paperback.

Kromdijk, G., *200 House Plants in Colour* (London: Lutterworth Press, 1970) 224 pp.; 200 excellent colour photographs.

Poincelot, Raymond P., *Gardening Indoors with House Plants* (Emmaus, Pa.: Rodale Press, 1974) 280 pp., paperback.

Index

123

English Ivy (*Hedera helix*), 25-6, 98-9
Episcia, 107
Erumpens (Palm), 90-1

F

Fallen plant, 39
Fatsia (Aralia), 106
Fertilizing, 70-2
Ficus benjamina, 93
Ficus elastica (Rubber Tree), 94-5
Fish fertilizer, 71, 98
Flowering Maple (*Abutilon*), 110-11
Fungi, 52
Fungus gnats, 51

G

Grape Ivy, 96

H

Hanging plants, 79, 84
Hedera helix (English Ivy), 25-6, 98-9
Holidays, 40-3
Humidity, 11,13-14, 72-5
—acclimatizing, 19-20
—atomizing, 14, 33
—misting, 14, 33
—winter and summer, 72-3

I

Insecticides, *see* Pesticides
Investigation, 11-12, 16-17
Ivy, 98-9

J

Jade Plant (*Crassula*),100-1
Jasmine, 109-10

K

Kangaroo Vine (*Cissus antarctica*), 110

L

Leaves, loss of, 38, 57-61
Light, 11, 13, 22-7
—artificial lighting, 84-8
—rotating (to give light), 32
—too little light, 27
—too much light, 27
—turning (to give light), 32
—window size (light intensity), 24
Lithops, 109
'Living Stone' plant (Lithops), 109

M

Marginata (Dracaena), 92
Mealybugs, 47-8
Mildew, 52
Millipedes, 51
Misting, 14, 33
Moulds, 52
Music (effect on plants), 114-15

N

Nephrolepsis exaltata bostoniensis (Boston Fern), 97-8

This book is set in 11/13 and 9/11 New Times Roman,
with subheadings in 11 pt bold. The chapter numbers
and titles are in 30 pt and 24 pt Elegante respectively.

1 2 3 4 5 6 7 8 9 10 WO 85 84 83 82 81 80 79 78 77 76